The Simple 6™ for Secondary Writers

by Kay Davidson

CLC0426
ISBN 978-1-934358-08-5

Marion IL
Cover by John Steele
www.piecesoflearning.com
Printed by Total Printing Systems
Newton, IL U.S.A.
05/2010

Dedication
to Bill, my favorite secondary teacher

Acknowledgements

Special thanks to:

All the teachers who submitted student writing samples from

Concord Junior High School
Concord High School
Elkhart Memorial High School
Kankakee Valley Middle School
Kankakee Valley High School
LaVille High School
Logansport High School
Logansport Learning Academy
Mishawaka High School
Mount Vernon High School
Pierre Moran Middle School
Sullivan High School
Wanatah Middle School

Kimberly Kieft and Tressa Decker, who edited and proofread.

Shirley Ross, who edited, proofread, and offered secondary advice.

Kathy Balsamo, my editor, for her expertise and guidance.

All the principals and superintendents who continue to send me data validating the success of this program.

Table of Contents

Chapter 1 

A Writing Rubric for Secondary Students

The Rationale

Based on the elementary and middle school academic standards for writing, The Simple 6™ gets straight to the heart of the matter in terms of expectations. This student-friendly, *simple analytic rubric* helps students and teachers focus on the components of exemplary writing – in the classroom and on standardized assessments.

While the NCTE offers guidelines for English teachers, there are no national academic standards for writing. Every state has designed its own set of standards and formal assessment, and most states offer a *complex holistic rubric* as their writing assessment tool. A complex holistic rubric is designed to assess many aspects of the writing at once, with the scorer finding the score point line that best fits the piece. Each segment of the rubric has a phrase, question, or narrative that defines the point value. Some states add the points from two individual scorers or place the point value into a mathematical equation that will eventually become a total language arts score.

This is what The Simple 6™ would look like if it were a complex holistic rubric.

The Simple 6™: A Writing Rubric for Students

	1 Poor	3 Minimal	5 Competent	6 Exemplary	Total
Focuses on the Topic	Attempts to focus on topic	Focuses on the topic	Focuses on the topic	Completely focuses on the topic	
Logical Order	Lacks order	Has logical order	Has an inviting beginning, descriptive body, and strong conclusion	Has fluent transitions, order that enhances meaning, an inviting introduction, and a powerful conclusion	
Challenging Vocabulary	Lacks challenging vocabulary	Attempts challenging vocabulary	Uses some challenging vocabulary	Uses concise, challenging vocabulary	
Sentence Patterns	Lacks varied sentence patterns	Sentences have list-like quality	Varies sentence patterns	Varies sentence patterns to enhance fluency	
Supporting Details	Lacks details	Lacks in-depth details	Has fully developed supporting details	Has fully developed, exceptional supporting details	
Audience	No audience connection	No audience connection	Tone and style are appropriate	Tone and voice make audience connection	
				Total	

Scoring student writing with a complex holistic rubric is difficult!

Why? Teachers give these reasons: The language is too ambiguous. . . It is too difficult to understand exactly how to move from one level to the next. . . Scoring takes too much time. . . Choosing the line in the rubric that "best fits" doesn't always give a true assessment. . . I need an assessment tool that will help me guide instruction, not just give me an approximation of my students' academic progress. . . So other than "following the exact format that is used in standardized assessment", what is accomplished by asking teachers (especially non-English teachers) to use complex holistic rubrics when they aren't comfortable with the process or the result? What is the real purpose of a rubric?

Rubrics are designed for two purposes: (1) to assess performance
(2) to articulate expectations

The term *rubric* is so often tied to assessment that teachers often forget to use a rubric to guide expectations. The key to developing The Simple 6™ was identifying the components of exemplary writing found in student writing samples that received high scores on standardized assessments. Learning to focus on the components in the assessment rubric instantly improved my students standardized test scores, but it also made them outstanding writers overall. If teachers will carefully articulate expectations, students will learn to write to those expectations.

How does The Simple 6™ help students improve their writing skills?

The key to education is understanding. Successful teachers focus on getting students to understand concepts rather than their being recipients of information that is delivered through lecture. The Simple 6™ is effective because students and teachers understand it. The language is clear, the order is developmentally progressive, and the scoring is relatively uncomplicated. Each component builds on the next, allowing students to master skills as they cumulatively review and work together to take control of their writing. Wherever you live, these elements of exemplary writing will be found or inferred on your state scoring rubric.

Focus on the topic.

Check for logical order.

Use challenging vocabulary.

Create varied sentence patterns.

Include exceptional supporting details.

Display a strong sense of audience or style.

What about high school, where the academic focus surpasses these strategies?

In a perfect world, all students would have mastered the basic language arts standards by the time they enter high school. That's what the standards say should have been accomplished. In actuality, however, there are some students who write proficiently, some students who don't come close to writing proficiently, and those students who have average or above-average skills, but don't focus on components being assessed. Because of their lack of focus, they receive non-passing scores on writing assessments, making it appear that their skills are below standard expectations. In reality, it may be that their writing skills are not deficient. They just didn't focus on what was being assessed.

As English teachers, it is important to remember that even high school students learn at different rates and come to writing class at a myriad of different cognitive levels. If secondary teachers insist on teaching at Level 10 when most students are functioning at Level 6, frustration and apathy will most likely prevail. If students are motivated to write and remediation skills are based on deficiencies seen in their writing samples, there is a higher likelihood of success. Use The Simple 6™ as your guide.

The Importance of Baseline Writing Samples

Collect a baseline sample from every student on the first day of class—no matter what subject you teach. Content-area teachers should consider choosing a topic that relates to the subject, even using it as a pretest. Just remember that students need a prior knowledge base. Students can write about a subject-related topic you know they have already studied such as photosynthesis, animal behavior, events in history, or mathematical procedures. More general topics such as safety, citizenship, academic achievement, responsibility, peer pressure, or career choice might also be used. Writing descriptive paragraphs about something simple like an apple, a memorable TV commercial, or a certain type of car are also effective; and don't forget the old standbys such as family, friends, goals, or pets. If the topic is appropriate for their age and interests, they will write. Just do it!

The most important thing to remember is that students at the secondary level will be coming to you from many levels of writing expertise. If these students are new to you, that baseline writing sample will provide invaluable information about the students' attitudes, overall language arts abilities, listening skills, attention to detail and neatness, and their ability to follow a short assignment through to completion.

In addition to giving you information about individual students, the writing sample can be used as a jump-start indicator of the types of skills you will need to teach as mini lessons to the entire class. Even in classes that are tracked for above-average students, there is always room for improvement. If students receive perfect scores on the first try, use them as examples and proceed accordingly. Students may be such outstanding writers that this year's goal will be to have every student publish something in a professional journal. Don't feel that a perfect score cannot or should not be given on the baseline. Outstanding, talented writers should certainly be rewarded for their efforts. Just don't forget to remind students that even essays with perfect scores can be revised and improved.

The most valuable use for the first-day writing sample is for students to realize their own growth throughout the semester. Give the assignment on the first day of school, collect it, analyze the information, and don't mention it to students for several weeks. After they have become familiar with three or four parts of The Simple 6™, amaze them by returning their original essay. Give them time to read it carefully, identifying the number of obvious components they "left out" of their original piece. Many may even want to use that piece as a springboard for revision and bring it to completion later in the year.

Students in Alternative Programs

Students in alternative programs may be coming and going in a "revolving door program" or be working within a more individualized curriculum. If students are working independently, they should check in with the teacher for instruction on each component. After conferencing, opportunities for guided practice, and assessment, they would move on to the next assignment. Whether instruction is being delivered to a large group (such as a night class for GED preparation), in small groups for students at similar skill levels, or individually – the instruction must occur. Start with *Focus on the Topic*, making sure that students always understand what they are supposed to write about. Teach them to use the prompt, focusing on the important parts. This will keep struggling readers from being overwhelmed and intimidated by the task before they even begin. Once students have mastered focusing on the topic, proceed to logical order. Give them plenty of opportunities to practice these ideas on a smaller scale, to ask questions, and to respond to the models that were used in the lesson.

Modification for Students with Varying Abilities

The only difference between *The Simple 6™ for Kids* and *The Simple 6™ for Secondary Students* is the level of sophistication by which the components are presented. Students with cognitive disabilities need more explanation, a slower pace, and more practice on each component. Don't sell those students short, though. They can master The Simple 6™ and have shown tremendous growth in their writing because of the concrete nature of the strategies. The elementary rubric is on the next page. If the language at that level is more appropriate for your students, use the elementary rubric instead of the rubric designed for secondary students.

Name ______________________________ Date __________

Story Title ___________________________ Score __________

The Simple 6™ A Writing Rubric for Kids

Stick to the topic.
Check for logical order.
Include interesting words.
Use different sentence patterns.
Create descriptive sentences.
Write for an audience.

Ask these questions:

yes/no

_____ Did you **stick to the topic**, or did you run away with some other idea?

_____ Have you presented your thoughts in a **logical order** that included an inviting beginning and a strong conclusion?

_____ Have you overused generic vocabulary, or have you gone back to look for opportunities to use **interesting words**?

_____ Did you use **different sentence patterns**, or does your story sound like a list?

_____ Does each paragraph have a topic sentence and supporting detail **sentences that are descriptive**?

_____ Did you write for an **audience**?
(being original, lively, or using another unique perspective appropriate for the prompt)

_____ **TOTAL POINTS** (How many did you answer yes?)

Name ______________________________ **Date** __________

Essay Title __________________________ **Score** __________

™ *A Writing Rubric for Secondary Students*

Focus on the topic.
Check for logical order.
Use challenging vocabulary.
Create varied sentence patterns.
Include exceptional supporting details.
Display a strong sense of audience.

Ask these questions:

1 / 0

_____ Did you **focus on the topic**, or did you run away with some other idea?

_____ Have you presented your thoughts in a **logical order** with an inviting introduction, a strong conclusion, and smooth transitions?

_____ Have you used **challenging vocabulary** to make descriptions rich and explanations detailed and precise?

_____ Have you created **varied sentence patterns** that contribute to the overall fluency of the piece?

_____ Did you include **exceptional supporting details** that address all the specific points of the prompt and include writers' techniques such as imagery, dialogue, humor, suspense, etc.?

_____ Did you write for a specific **audience**?
(Did you write with an original, lively, authoritative tone; or did you use any other unique perspective that made a direct connection with the audience?)

_____ TOTAL POINTS

A Review of The Simple 6™: Question Format

Focus on the Topic

Did I focus on the topic and not run away with other ideas?
Did I answer all the questions in the prompt or assignment?
If there were no questions, did I create my own?

Logical Order

Is there an introduction, or did I just dive right into the body?
Did I use a lead or hook to get my readers interested?
Is the body organized, probably by the questions in the prompt?
Did each paragraph address a new question?
If the task did not include questions, did I develop my own?
Is my conclusion strong? Is it more than one sentence?

Challenging Vocabulary

Did I eliminate overused words such as *went, said, big, little, good, awesome*, etc.?
Did I go back and look for opportunities to use other challenging vocabulary?
Are the new words used correctly?

Varied Sentence Patterns

Does my essay or story sound like a list?
Did I vary my sentence patterns, using questions and exclamations?
Did I put items in a series?
Did I focus primarily on the use of compound and/or complex sentences?
Did I effectively use prepositional phrases, adverbs, and participial phrases?
Does my use of varied sentence patterns contribute to the overall fluency of the piece?

Exceptional Supporting Details

Did I use precise verbs?
Did I name people, places, and things with proper nouns?
Did I include adjectives – but not too many?
Did I use imagery and other literary devices to create a clear vision of my thoughts?
Did I give several detailed examples that supported my topic sentence?

Audience/Voice

Did I write with an original, lively, or authoritative tone that was appropriate for the prompt?
Did I use any other unique perspective that made a direct connection with the audience?
Does my personality shine through my writing?

The Simple 6™ for Secondary Students

Focus on the Topic

- Focus on the topic and don't run away with other ideas.
- Follow the prompt instructions.

Logical Order

- BME (beginning, middle, end)
- Focus on the inviting introduction and the strong conclusion.
- Use the prompt to guide structure.

Challenging Vocabulary

- Include a minimum of three challenging vocabulary attempts.
- Eliminate generic words such as went, said, big, little, good, etc.
- Use new words correctly.

Varied Sentence Patterns

- Include questions, exclamations. and items in a series.
- Focus on complex sentences.
- Use dialogue, if appropriate.
- Use sentence patterns to make writing fluent.

Exceptional Supporting Details

- Use precise verbs.
- Include proper nouns.
- Insert adjectives - not too many.
- Use a variety of literary techniques.

Audience/Voice

- Write in a tone that is appropriate for the prompt.
- Make a direct connection to the audience.
- Let your personality shine!

Chapter 2 Writing in English Class

The academic standards for writing tell secondary English teachers that they should be focusing on higher level thinking and literary skills such as reflection, analysis and more advanced literary techniques. Because many students have not mastered the writing standards along the way, however, teachers sometimes have no choice but to step back and remediate students in basic writing skills.

Meeting secondary students at their current cognitive level and moving forward from there is just as important in the middle and high school as it is at the elementary level. While the standards tell us that all writing skills should have been mastered by Grade 8, it is more a goal than a reality. Heterogeneous grouping of students with diverse levels of writing performance and rigorous state standards also complicate the teaching of writing. Meeting the needs of all students is a daunting challenge for teachers, but The Simple 6™ makes a difference for all students.

Further complicating the issue is high school scheduling. Many high schools still offer isolated classes in vocabulary, grammar, literature, and writing. During the past ten years, extensive research in literacy has changed language arts teaching at the elementary level. Young students are learning to analyze, reflect, and respond to what they are reading or experiencing in life. Yet, at the secondary level, literacy skills are traditionally taught in isolation.

By the time students reach high school, they have received writing instruction within all literary genres. They should have had extensive experience in writing reports, presentations, research papers, and expository, narrative, descriptive, and persuasive essays. Why then, do so many high school students fail to produce exemplary writing samples on short, standardized writing assessments?

Here are five basic reasons to consider:

1) Students aren't familiar with using the information provided in the prompt.
2) The finished pieces lack structure that show students "attacked" the prompt.
3) Students don't understand how much content is required to show "evidence of mastery" of standards-based skills.
4) Students don't seem to have a cache of strategies to promote descriptive writing.
5) Their writing isn't readable, so it doesn't really matter what they write.

The Simple 6™ won't help students to improve their penmanship, but it will help them focus on structure and the components of exemplary writing. While the ideas behind the program are at the elementary level, many students have obviously forgotten some of the skills along the way. An organized, concise review of The Simple 6™ in one grading period will help students to focus on assessment criteria, teach them how to structure their writing, and provide them with a relatively short list of revision strategies. In addition, the program helps students write within a specific time frame, which is important in on-demand prompt writing.

Implementation: 9 Weeks or 6 Weeks?

The program is designed to be implemented in nine weeks. For six-week grading periods or rotations, consider compacting or integrating weeks 4, 8, and 9. The alternative, of course, is to continue into the next grading period if necessary. Here is an overview of the activities.

Start: Make student writing folders. *(cover template is provided)*
Collect a baseline writing sample from each student. *(prompts in Ch.3)*
Score. Complete Class Analysis Chart and Quarterly Tracking Chart.

Week 1: Focus on the Topic
Don't run away with other ideas.
Follow the prompt instructions.

Week 2: Logical Order
Introduce Prompt Attack to develop body paragraphs.
Review strategies for introduction and conclusion.

Week3: Challenging Vocabulary
Identify overused words.
Revise using new words correctly.

Week 4: Review Week (Optional)
Introduce Prompt Attack for What-Why prompts.

Week 5: Varied Sentence Patterns
Review questions, exclamations, and items in a series.
Simplify the concept of complex sentences.

Week 6: Exceptional Supporting Details
Insert precise verbs, proper nouns, and powerful adjectives.
Use imagery or other literary techniques (per standards).

Week 7: Audience/Voice
Develop the appropriate tone.
Use voice to connect with the audience.

Week 8: Scoring
Practice and discuss.

Week 9: Revision Strategies
Attack it! Simple 6™ it! Practice and discuss.

Finish: Collect a final writing sample from each student.

My Writing Record

DATE	TITLE	SCORE

Week 1: Focus on the Topic — Day 1

Title: ***Don't Run Away With Other Ideas*** **Time:** 60 minutes

Behavioral Objectives: Students will:

- identify sentences that do not focus on topic
- work in small groups for revision

Academic Standards: Establish a coherent thesis that maintains focus throughout. Revise to improve logic.

Materials Needed: student writing samples

Introduction:

Today we are going to start a writing program called The Simple 6™. There are 6 individual components that we are going to study. The first component is ***called Focus on the Topic. Focus on the Topic*** *has two parts.*

- *Focus on the topic, and don't run away with other ideas.*
- *Follow the prompt instructions.*

Lesson:

Let's talk about not running away with other ideas. What does this mean?

Share the first student writing sample with students (*next page*). Ask students to critique the writing. Do they notice that there are sentences that don't belong? Discuss and substitute sentences that will give the paragraph more fluency.

Guided Practice:

Have students work in small groups to revise the second sample, making sure all sentences focus on the topic. Then, if time, share results with the whole group.

Conclusion:

As you write, make sure that you don't run away with other ideas. In other words, don't include sentences that are not related to this topic.

Assessment:

Students will eliminate sentences in future writing that do not focus on the topic.

Reflection:

Writing Task #1: Identify a lesson you learned from watching the play "The Crucible."

I watched the play, "The Crucible." I have learned many things. I think that could lead you into some bad things. I have once been a follower a long time ago. Thinking you would fit in with the popular kids. The only person you should try to be is yourself. You don't need to be someone else just to fit in. Half the time it will lead you to bad things from doing it. This happened when I was younger.

Writing Task #2: If you could meet any famous person, whom would you choose?

The famous person I would choose to meet with is Abe Lincoln. He's honest, trust worthy, and tall. I would meet in the White House, of course. First he would take me on a tour, then we would probably have lunch, and then he would show me his office. Too bad he gets shot in the head while watching a play. He went to the Ford Theatre with his wife, and that was the end of him. That would be the day I would remember the most, I think.

Week 1: Focus on the Topic — Day 2

Title: ***Follow Instructions*** — **Time: 60 minutes**

Behavioral Objectives: Students will:
- review prompt format
- outline prompt structure
- work in small groups to identify title / questions

Academic Standards: Select a focus and organization structure.
Establish a coherent thesis that maintains focus throughout.
Identify the topic and develop ideas.

Materials Needed: secondary prompt (provided)

Introduction:

Review: *Yesterday we started a writing program called The Simple 6™. There are six individual components we are going to learn about. What is the first one?*

***Focus on the Topic. Focus on the Topic** has two parts. What are they?*

(Students respond verbally without looking at review sheet in Chapter 1. *Don't run away with ideas* and *follow directions.*)

Share the prompt on the following page (or one from a previous assessment) with students. Review prompt format.

Lesson:

Ask students to outline the structure of a typical prompt.

Anticipated Response: Title

P1	Scenario / Questions / Information
P2	Task / Repeated Questions in Sentence Format
P3	Reminder Box / Bulleted Questions

Guided Practice:

Share another prompt with students. (*See samples in Chapter 3*)

Have students work in small groups to identify the title and the questions that would make up the body paragraphs.

Conclusion:

Answer questions that students may have about following the instructions on the prompt.

Assessment:

Informal Observation

Reflection:

Name ______________________ **Writing Sample**
Teacher ______________________ **Middle School GR** ___
Date ______________________ **SCORE:**

Letter to a Parent

Read the writing prompt below and complete the writing activity.

Teenagers typically think that their parents don't listen to them—and usually don't agree with them. Do you communicate well with your parents? Is there an issue that has been on your mind? How can they help you work through it?

Write a letter to one or both of your parents. Discuss how you feel about the level of communication you have with them. Tell them about an issue that has been on your mind. Ask for their help in working through this issue.

Be sure to:

plan your letter before you begin.
include an introduction, a body, and a strong conclusion.
focus on the following ideas:
your level of communication
an issue that has been bothering you
how your parents can help
include exceptional supporting details.

Your writing will not be scored on your personal opinions. It will be scored objectively on:

- *how clearly you address the prompt*
- *how well you organize your ideas*
- *how effectively you express yourself*
- *how consistently you use correct paragraphing, grammar, spelling, and punctuation.*

Be sure to use the Standard Rules of English, which do not include slang or jargon.

Week 1

Writing Task #1: Write a letter to one or both of your parents that addresses an issue that is bothering you.

Dear Mother,

I write you today because I'm very pleased that you love me and treat me with the proper respect for someone my age. It pleases me to say that you are very nice and also an attentive listener. Furthermore, you should probably be qualified for an award or at the very least a pat on the back for taking your parenting responsibilities seriously. That's what I want to say to you.

Love, Joe

Writing Task #2:

Dear Mom,

I would like it if you would let me learn some things on my own. Everything I have ever done or said you have something bad to say about it. You don't trust me. You don't trust my friends, and I don't know what my friends and I have done to be untrustworthy! Every once and a while I wish you wouldn't say something about what I did. I'm not even sure you know who I am anymore. Some things I just don't tell you because I'm afraid of what you'll say. Some of my friends don't even want to come over because their afraid your going to judge them on everything they do. I don't think any of it is fair.

Makenzie

Week 2: Logical Order — Day 1

Title: ***BME: Prompt Attack***
Part I: Developing the Body of Your Essay

Time: 60 minutes

Behavioral Objectives: Students will:
- identify prompt questions
- develop body on Prompt Attack template

Academic Standards: Use graphic organizers to plan writing.
Revise to improve organization.
Develop main ideas.

Materials Needed: Prompt Attack template
Prompt sample (*next page*)

Introduction:
Review Focus on the Topic and its subcomponents.
Today we are moving on to the second component, ***Logical Order. Logical Order*** *is obviously based on the BME:* ***B****eginning,* ***M****iddle, and* ***E****nd. For our purposes they will be referred to as the introduction, body, and conclusion. Today we are going to focus on developing the body of your essay based on the questions in the prompt. This is Part I of Prompt Attack.*

Lesson:
Share a prompt (with questions) with students. Identify the questions in the prompt. Model the placement of these questions on Prompt Attack (on overhead or board). Answer the questions in complete sentences. Think about other details that might make up the remainder of the paragraph. Place key words next to asterisks. Answer all questions asked by students.

Guided Practice:
In pairs, let students work together to write questions on their individual Prompt Attack template. Questions should be answered in complete sentences. Key words should be written next to asterisks. Students should check over each other's work.

Conclusion:
Use the questions in the prompt to help you organize the body of your essay. The answer to each question will be the topic sentence for that paragraph. Later you will check to make sure these sentences are complex, but for right now focus on getting a topic sentence and key words that will give you ideas for developing supporting details.

Assessment:
Informal observation during work time. Check over papers.

Reflection:

Week 2

Writing Task #1: The Special Lunch

You have been given a rare opportunity. You may invite anyone you choose to a special lunch. Who would you invite? Where would the lunch be held? What would you talk about during lunch? How would meeting this person make you feel?

Write a real or imaginative essay about your special lunch. Be sure to include who would be invited, where you would go, what you would talk about, and how meeting this person would make you feel.

Student Writing Sample #1: Lunch with Old Friends
without Prompt Attack

If I had room at the lunch table, I would choose to have lunch with my old friends from my last school. I'm talking specifically about Krystal, sKayla, Yesenia, and Amy. You see, my parents wanted to build a new house in the country. That meant we had to move. I miss my old school so much that I would definitely choose those girls. I miss hanging out with them and all the things we used to talk about. I didn't realize it would be this hard to transfer to a new school and make new friends.

Prompt Sample 3-Question: The Lunch of a Lifetime *with Prompt Attack*

If I were able to pick one person to go to lunch with it would definitely be my great grandfather Wilson. I have never met him but from what I know about his personality and his interests, I think we would have a lot in common. Just seeing how amazing my great grandma Dorothy is, it makes me want to meet him even more.

He would probably enjoy eating in a quiet restaurant where we could hold a memorable conversation. I know I would prefer that intimate setting. The best place would be Papa Vino's. I really enjoy the delicious Italian food there, plus many tables are located in quiet corners.

As we ate, I would try not to besiege him with too many questions. Since he died when I was just three months old there are so many things I'd like to ask him. For instance: where he grew up, how old he was when he met Grandma, how they met, whether or not he attended college, the type of student he was, and how he decided on his occupation (which was dentistry). Even though these are questions I could ask Grandpa Tom, his son, or even Great Grandma Dorothy, it isn't quite the same.

Week 2

Meeting my grandfather would be absolutely unbelievable! Of course I realize this meeting would never be possible, but just imagining it fills a void. I know I would be excited and amazed to meet him because of all the wonderful things I've heard about him. We must have had a connection even when I was a baby, because I just can't make the wonder go away.

If I had the choice I would definitely have lunch with Grandpa. He was, after all, the founder of our family and its traditions. I spend reflective moments from time to time wishing I could remember meeting and spending time with him. Even though having those memories is not possible, imagining what it would have been like is really the next best thing. My special lunch date would really bring him to reality for me.

LEAD

The person I would want to have a special lunch with is my great grandfather Wilson. TITLE/TOPIC

Q 1: Where would the lunch be held?
He would probably enjoy eating in a quiet restaurant.

* memorable conversation
* intimate setting
* Papa Vino's
* Italian food

The Special Lunch

Q 2: What would we talk about during lunch?
Since he died when I was just three months old, there are many things I want to ask him.

* where he grew up
* how old when he met Grandma
* attend college?
* how he chose his occupation

Q 3: How would meeting this person make me feel?
Meeting my grandfather would be unbelievable.

* not possible
* imagine
* excited and amazed
* make the wonder go away

LEAD
SOLUTION
My special lunch date would really bring him to reality for me. REFLECTION

Week 2

TITLE/TOPIC

LEAD

Q 1:

* * * *

Q 2:

* * * *

Q 3:

* * * *

LEAD

SOLUTION

REFLECTION

Week 2: Logical Order — Day 2A

Title: ***Introduction and Conclusion*** **Time: 60 minutes**

PART A: Introduction *This lesson may need to be broken into 2 parts.*

Behavioral Objectives: Students will:
- review strategies for leads
- write an inviting introduction

Academic Standards: Choose appropriate techniques for an introduction.
Revise to improve organization.

Materials Needed: literature example with great introduction
Prompt Attack template

Introduction:
Student Review: **Focus on the Topic, Logical Order**
Prompt Attack Part II is developing an introduction. Part III is the conclusion.

Lesson:
Today we will talk about leads for an introduction. To find out which leads you've have had the most experience with, let's generate a list on the board. (Make sure final list covers all options. Depending on their backgrounds, unfamiliar lead strategies may have to be modeled and used throughout the year. List for review on the following page.)

Guided Practice:
Take a story students are familiar with, such as something recently read or a fairy tale. Have students write three different leads for the same story. Which leads turned out to be most appropriate? Why?

Conclusion:
Remember: The purpose for the introduction is to inform the reader of the topic and to get them interested enough to keep reading.

Assessment:
Have students share their "best of three" introductions. Students may offer positive comments or suggestions for improvement in small groups. Teacher will observe.

Reflection:

Introductions

Purpose:

- ***to inform the reader of the topic***
- ***to get the reader interested enough to continue reading***

A Short List of Common Leads

Anecdote
Start with a short story or narrative that sets the tone.

Analogy
Begin with like or as, making a direct comparison to an unrelated item or circumstance.

Definition
Get straight to the point by starting with an exact definition.

Description
Create a vivid picture of the setting, character, background, or mood. It may build up to the introduction of the topic.

Fact or Statistic
Start with a fact. Depending on the type of writing, this information may or may not be true.

Opinion
Common in persuasive writing, take a stand and support it with substantial reasons.

Question
Start with a question or series of questions that get the reader to start thinking or reflecting about the topic.

Quotation
Begin with a quotation, making sure it is relevant to the topic.

Word
Write one word that sets the tone or lets the reader know the topic.

Your Favorite Leads from Literature

Source:

Source:

Source:

Source:

Source:

Week 2: Logical Order — Day 2B

Title: ***Introduction and Conclusion***
PART B: Conclusion

Time: 60 minutes

Behavioral Objectives: Students will:
- review strategies for conclusions
- write a strong conclusion

Academic Standards: Choose appropriate techniques for a conclusion.
Revise to improve organization.

Materials Needed: Literature example with great conclusion
Prompt Attack template

Introduction:
Student Review: **Focus on the Topic, Logical Order**
Prompt Attack Part II is developing an introduction. Part III is the conclusion.

Lesson:
Yesterday we discussed many effective ways to begin an essay. Let's review them.
Today we will talk about conclusions. There are three main reasons for writing a strong conclusion:
- *to summarize or review your main points*
- *to solve a problem*
- *to give cause for reflection*

There are a number of strategies to consider when writing a conclusion. (Found on next page). The important thing to remember is to choose the one that is most effective for the type of paper you are writing.

Let's think for a moment about the story of The Three Little Pigs. You all know what happened. Mother Pig sent her three boys out into the world to seek their fortunes. They each built a house – one of straw, one of sticks, and one of stone. Once the wolf discovered that he could not blow the last pig's house down, what happened? Take five minutes to write a strong conclusion to this story.

Guided Practice:
Take out your Prompt Attack in progress. Complete the conclusion.

Conclusion:
Each of you will receive a handout today that reviews the steps of Prompt Attack. Put it in your writing notebook for future use.

Assessment:
Self-assessment. Which strategies were most effective?

Reflection:

Conclusions

Purpose: ***to summarize or review***
to solve a problem
to give cause for reflection

Strategies for Conclusions

Anecdote
End with a short story that brings the writing full circle.

Analogy
End with like or as, making a direct comparison to an unrelated item or circumstance.

Elaboration
Spend some time on your conclusion, making sure that it is more than one sentence. Eliminate "THE END".

Open
Close with a hint of things to come.

Opinion
Common in persuasive writing, strongly reiterate the stand taken throughout the paper.

Question
Close with a question or series of questions that cause the reader to reflect or create an opinion.

Quotation
End with a quotation, making sure it is dynamic and thought-provoking.

Reflection
Close with a personal comment or reflection.

Solution
Solve the mystery or resolve the problem.

Summary
Review the main ideas of your essay.

Surprise
Finish with an idea that was totally unexpected by the reader.

Week 2

Your Favorite Conclusions from Literature

Source:

Source:

Source:

Source:

Source:

Prompt Attack Review for Secondary Students

Think about time and materials.
Do you know when you have to be finished?
Do you have all the planning paper you need?

Focus on the title.
What is your essay going to be about?

Read the prompt carefully.
What type of prompt is it? (3-Question? What - Why?)
How will you structure it?

Design the Prompt Attack graphic organizer.

BODY
Put the title in the center in an oval.
Web the questions from the prompt.
Answer them in complete sentences (that you will later make complex).
Put key words or ideas next to the asterisks to develop relevant supporting details.

INTRODUCTION
At least refer to the title or state the topic of your paper.
If possible, create a lead to get your readers interested.

CONCLUSION
Lead into the conclusion.
Solve the problem OR give an overview of ideas or reasons.
State your opinion, feelings, or reflect on something you still wonder about.

Write your rough draft.
Focus on fully developed paragraphs that provide examples and detailed descriptions.

Reread your essay.
Review your Prompt Attack organizer, making sure you have followed directions.
Proofread for sentence fluency and idea completion.
Edit for errors in capitalization, punctuation, spelling, and subject/verb agreement.
Make sure you wrote enough – always more than one page.
Write neatly and large enough so your writing can be read easily.

Week 3: Challenging Vocabulary — Day 1

Title: ***Identify Overused Words*** **Time: 60 minutes**

Behavioral Objectives: Students will:

- eliminate overused words from their writing
- use synonyms to improve vocabulary

Academic Standards: Revise to improve word choice.
Use varied and expanded vocabulary.

Materials Needed: List of 10 overused words
2 x 3 scrap paper

Introduction:

Review the Simple 6™ components: **Focus on the Topic, Logical Order.**
Number your paper from 1-5. Think of the words you overuse most often in your writing. List them.

Lesson:

Today we will review the use of synonyms and how to use a thesaurus. Remember as you choose substitutions for overused words, it is imperative that you use the new words correctly. They are not just for show. Reread your essay to make sure meaning has not been lost and that subjects and verbs are in agreement.

Guided Practice:

Let students work in groups to establish lists of synonyms for the most overused words. Write them on the templates provided on the following pages.

Conclusion:

Improvement of vocabulary is many times the first step in revision, because in writing a draft the concern is getting the ideas down - not necessarily getting them down in final form. Always remember to reread your writing, looking for opportunities to improve the level of vocabulary.

Assessment:

All students participated and created a list of synonyms for their most overused words.

Reflection:

Writing Task: Excerpt from Narrative Essay
Overused and Low-level Vocabulary

. . .The next day I decided to tell my brother about this dream I had about a ghost, and he told me that it couldn't be real. That night we decided that we would go and try to see this ghost. The girls had decided that they would go with us, but they decided they weren't going to get out of the vehicle. We went to the church and this time it was around midnight and it was raining which made it just as scary as in the dream. We decided to drive around the church, took the keys, and sat them in front of the same grave as the night before. As we went back to the car we heard a man screaming and decided he must be in trouble. We turned around and I saw the ghost from the night before. I was speechless! I couldn't decide if he was real or not..

We haven't returned to that church since the night we saw the ghosts, but the memory still haunts us. We have heard about other people that experienced the same thing as us. We have decided that most people just don't believe it happened. I am here to tell you that all of us saw a ghost - in the dream and in real life!

List the overused words:

Improvement Strategies:

Week 3

Frequently Overused Words

Synonyms for *WENT*

____________	____________	____________
____________	____________	____________
____________	____________	____________
____________	____________	____________
____________	____________	____________

Synonyms for *SAID*

____________	____________	____________
____________	____________	____________
____________	____________	____________
____________	____________	____________
____________	____________	____________

Synonyms for *BIG*

____________	____________	____________
____________	____________	____________
____________	____________	____________
____________	____________	____________
____________	____________	____________

Frequently Overused Words

Synonyms for _______________

Synonyms for _______________

Synonyms for _______________

Week 3: Challenging Vocabulary — Day 2

Title: ***Using Synonyms to Increase Vocabulary Level*** **Time: 60 minutes**

Behavioral Objectives: Students will:

- revise to increase vocabulary

Academic Standards: Revise to improve word choice.
Use varied and expanded vocabulary.
Use extended vocabulary.

Materials Needed: student sample with overused words

Introduction:

A student leads the review of **Focus on the Topic, Logical Order,** and **Challenging Vocabulary.** Make sure all students can recite the components and subcomponents from memory. (Leader may use review sheet.)

Any questions about the components we have studied this far? Any questions in particular about the exercise we did yesterday in which you found synonyms by using a thesaurus?

Lesson:

Today we are going to use synonyms to improve the overall quality of a piece of writing. (Provide students with a secondary writing sample from a student in another class or from the next page.)

Guided Practice:

Read the essay. Then work with a partner to identify the overused words by circling them. Replace the overused words with the appropriate synonyms, making sure they are used correctly in context.

Conclusion:

Remember, most people do not typically write with higher level vocabulary when they write their first draft. This is usually something that is done in the initial stages of revision. It is the easiest revision strategy. Don't forget to check for overused words.

Assessment:

Ask students to turn in revised papers to be scored or have them share revised samples in large or small groups.

Reflection:

Writing Task: Write an essay that describes how you will help your cousin find the perfect pair of jeans.

Student Writing Sample #1: How to Buy a Pair of Jeans

My cousin has just moved in with me, but her clothes are not very good for the school she will attend. Today we are going to the mall to find a good pair of jeans. We both agree on shopping in department stores where there is a big selection for a cheap price. We go to JC Pennys to find a good pair that are not as tight as the ones she already has. Some were too big. Others were way too little. We thought we would never find a good pair. We went to two other stores and finally we found a good pair of jeans. They were faded, but not too much. They were not too low or tight, which is just what we were hoping for. She really looked good in them. My cousin cannot wait for the first day of school, so she can wear her new jeans.

Week 3

Student Sample #2: **How to Buy the Perfect Pair of Jeans**

My cousin Luci, from New Orleans, came to live with my family and me. She doesn't have any nice clothes that I feel would be right for my school though. Later on we will go to the mall and buy her a nice pair of blue jeans. because that is the best place to buy just about anything, especially a pair of blue jeans. There just so many stores and name brand companies. It is hard to choose the best one. In my opinion, though, Old Navy has the best brand of jeans.

They should look good on you with whatever you wear with them. They should be a little bit faded. They should also be one or two sizes too big so that they aren't plastered to your legs. Also, make sure they aren't too short or people will make fun of you.

My cousin finally found the best pair of jeans . Hopefully, everyone at school will think she looks nice.

Week 4: Review Week — Day 1

Title: ***Review 3-Question Prompt: Prompt Attack*** **Time: 60 minutes**

Behavioral Objectives: Students will:
- review Prompt Attack structure with a 3-Question Prompt

Academic Standards: Organize the composition.
Use graphic organizers to plan writing.

Materials Needed: 3-Question Prompt
3-Question Prompt Attack template
Computer with overhead projection

Introduction:
Student review of Simple 6™ components.

Lesson:
Today we will review how to attack a prompt. Who remembers the purpose for doing this? A few weeks ago we learned how to attack a prompt with different questions. Just to make sure you still remember how to do it, you will be attacking a 3-Question Prompt individually. We will then use our planning pages to write an essay together. One of you will be leading that writing lesson.

Guided Practice:
Students will work as a class to contribute ideas to Prompt Attack on overhead. One student will then lead the class in developing an essay response based on Prompt Attack notes.

Conclusion:
Remember, in a 3-Question Prompt, all the questions are different. The purpose of answering each question is to develop a topic sentence that will be supported by exceptional details. These questions should always relate directly to the prompt.

Assessment:
Observation of student participation. Collecting the Prompt Attacks is optional.

Reflection:

Week 4: Review Week — Day 2

Title: ***Attack a What-Why Prompt*** **Time: 60 minutes**

Behavioral Objectives: Students will:

- attack a What-Why Prompt

Academic Standards: Identify the topic and organize ideas.
Organize the composition.
Use graphic organizers to plan writing.

Materials Needed: What-Why Prompt
What-Why Prompt Attack template
Choose prompts from Chapter 3 or design your own.

Introduction:

Student review of Simple 6™ components.

Today we are going to focus on the What - Why prompt. This type of prompt asks you to choose something and give reasons why you made your choice.

Lesson:

Today you will be working in groups to attack a What-Why Prompt. First we will take a look at a What-Why prompt and a Prompt Attack template for that type of prompt. In a What-Why prompt you are being asked to make a choice and give reasons in fully developed paragraphs. The teacher will explain the City Project prompt, making sure students understand how to use the information provided. Student samples with and without Prompt Attack will follow.

Guided Practice:

Students will work with a partner to attack a different What-Why prompt.
Discuss results together as a class.

Conclusion:

Remember, the main difference between attacking a 3 Question Prompt and a What-Why Prompt is that in a 3 Question you are answering 3 different questions from the prompt. In a What-Why you are making a choice and supporting it with 3 reasons.

Assessment:

Reflection:

The City Project

Your mayor has put a huge ad in the paper inviting the public to state their opinions on which of the following projects should be financed. Three are being considered, but there is only enough money to finance one project. The choices are:

a nature center that would include areas for hiking, camping, supervised nature walks, and an environmental activity center for elementary-age children

an animal shelter that would provide temporary homes for unwanted animals, classes about pet care, and adoption services

a library on wheels that would provide books, DVDs, and music CDs to those citizens who are unable to travel to the public library

a technology school that would offer reasonably-priced classes for residents age 12 and up in computers, digital photography, cell phones, and high definition TV-DVDs.

Write a persuasive essay to be submitted to the mayor that explains the city project that you think would most benefit the residents of your town.

Pre-writing Activity Format

Be sure to:
plan your writing before you begin.
include an introduction, supportive reasons, and a conclusion.
address the following points of the prompt:
the city project you think will be most beneficial reasons why
include specific supporting details to make your essay persuasive

Week 4

Here is a student's essay before knowing how to attack a prompt.

If you want my opinion, I think we should build an animal shelter. There are so many unwanted animals in our town it is getting way out of hand, not to mention dangerous. The children aren't safe and the pound is catching all the stray dogs and putting them to sleep. It is so wrong to do that to o a poor defenseless animal. It isn't their fault nobody wants them. They need love and care, and that is why I say the animal shelter should be the number one choice for the city project.

This is the same essay, written after attacking the prompt.

I recently read the ad asking for opinions about which project will most benefit the residents of our city. I feel strongly that an animal shelter has been needed for a very long time. My reasons are that there are too many strays running through town, they need care, and if we had a more organized adoption program, not as many would be put to sleep. Let me go into more detail.

Have you noticed the number of unwanted animals roaming the streets in town? They are very dangerous to children walking home from school. They are also a nuisance to restaurant owners whose trash cans they dump over looking for food. These animals have been neglected by their owners and if nobody wants them they are put to sleep.

These animals just need care. They search for food wherever they can, making messes in the process. They also need shelter, especially in winter. Many of them have not had the proper shots and may be carrying rabies. Someone needs to be available to offer pet care classes for new pet owners.

The number of pets being put to sleep bothers me. The animal shelter could sponsor Adoption Night, or could put pictures of featured pets in the newspaper each week. A weekly notice in the paper could allow more families to get pets for a cheaper price than at a pet store. The main advantage, though, would be that fewer pets would be put to sleep.

I've lived in this town for many years, and I'm here to tell you that it's time we had an animal shelter. Please consider saving these poor, defenseless animals. I know you'll do the right thing!

LEAD

The city project should be a new animal shelter. TITLE/TOPIC

WHY 1: *(too many unwanted animals)*

* *roaming the streets*
* *dangerous to children*
* *being neglected*
* *being put to sleep*

City Project

WHY 2: *(need care)*

* *food*
* *shelter*
* *shots*
* *attention*

WHY 3: *(could be adopted)*

* *adoption night*
* *newspaper pictures*
* *new pet for a cheap price*
* *fewer pets being put to sleep*

LEAD

SUMMARY

Please consider saving these poor, defenseless animals! REFLECTION

LEAD
TITLE/TOPIC

WHY 1:

*
*
*
*

WHY 3:

*
*
*
*

WHY 2:

*
*
*
*

LEAD
SUMMARY
REFLECTION

Week 5: Varied Sentence Patterns — Day 1

Title: ***Kinds of Sentences*** **Time: 60 minutes**

Behavioral Objectives: Students will:

- review sentences classified by purpose
- review sentences classified by structure.
- examine the seven sentence patterns.

Academic Standards: Revise to create varied sentence patterns.
Revise to create fluency.

Materials Needed: Student paragraph written in declarative sentences only.

Introduction:

Student review of Simple 6™ components.
Classified by purpose, what are the four kinds of sentences?
(declarative, interrogative, imperative, and exclamatory)
Classified by structure, what are the four kinds of sentences?
(simple, compound, complex, and compound-complex)
There are seven basic sentence patterns. What are they?
(see next page)

Lesson:

(Show student paragraph.) *How many kinds of sentences do you see based on purpose? . . . based on structure? How many different patterns can you identify?*

Guided Practice:

(Students will work in groups of three.) *Choose one of the paragraphs provided. Revise one paragraph, focusing first on the kinds of sentences that you see. Next, concentrate on sentence patterns. Once your revisions are complete, recopy the paragraph--every other line – on another sheet of paper. It must be brought to class tomorrow, because we are going to continue to revise this piece.*

Conclusion:

Don't always feel like you have to TELL everything you know when you write. Think about wondering, reflecting, and showing excitement in your writing. Include short and long sentences to avoid choppy, list-like writing.

Assessment:

Observe group interaction and student participation.

Reflection:

Reviewing Sentences

Sentences Classified by Purpose: 4 Kinds

*It's important to do more than **tell** things in your writing. Use all kinds of sentences. Ask questions. Show excitement!*

declarative: a statement
interrogative: a question
imperative: a command
exclamatory: an exclamation

Sentences Classified by Structure: 4 Kinds

Try to avoid using too many short S-V sentences. Combine different kinds and lengths of sentences to make your writing more fluent.

simple:	one independent clause
compound:	two or more independent clauses
complex:	one independent clause and at least one subordinate clause
compound-complex:	two or more independent clauses and at least one subordinate clause

Sentence Patterns: 7 Kinds

Vary your sentence patterns to make your writing more interesting.

S-V	Subject / Verb People eat.
S-V-DO	Subject / Verb / Direct Object People eat food.
S-V-IO-DO	Subject / Verb / Indirect Object / Direct Object Mary gave them dinner.
S-V-DO-OC(A)	Subject / Verb / Direct Object / Object Complement (adjective) Dinner made the people happy.
S-V-DO-OC(N)	Subject / Verb / Direct Object / Object Complement (noun) They called Mary a master chef.
S-LV-PN	Subject / Linking Verb / Predicate Nominative She is an excellent cook.
S-LV-PA	Subject / Linking Verb / Predicate Adjective Mary was pleased.

Week 5

Writing Task:	***Write a paragraph describing how you feel on the opening day of a new school year.***

Student Writing Sample #1

I just want to say that I enjoyed the opening day of school this year. I saw a lot of friends who I didn't see much of this summer. I also met a lot of new friends who were pretty nice. I'm looking forward to this year. I'm wanting to get closer to a close friend of mine. I was also excited to see who was in my classes. I will miss sleeping in, but I hope I will enjoy my junior year.

Writing Task:	***Write about the person in your life that you consider to be the most special.***

Student Writing Sample #2

I just want to tell you that the special person I have chosen is my dad. I have chosen him because I am thankful for all the things he does for me. He has never thought of me as his foster son but always his biological son. He means a lot to me because he has always been there for me when I needed help. He has also taught me numerous things that I will need to know in the future. He also has small engine repair skills that he has taught me. He can fix our car if the transmission is down or anything like that. He has outstanding qualities. He is always content around other people, and he can cheer me up when I am feeling depressed. I hope he realizes how much he means to me.

Week 5: Varied Sentence Patterns — Day 2

Title: ***Using Clauses and Phrases to Enhance Fluency*** **Time: 60 minutes**

Behavioral Objectives: Students will:

- vary sentence structure.
- revise sentence beginnings.
- focus on sentence fluency.

Academic Standards: Revise to improve sentence variety.

Materials Needed: Handouts on the following pages

Introduction:

Student review of Simple 6™ components.

Lesson:

What is the difference between a clause and a phrase? (see next page)
What are the two types of clauses?
How many different types of phrases are there? Let's list them on the board.
Give students the handout on the following page to review clauses and phrases.

Because there are so many strategies related to sentence variety, sentence structure, and sentence patterns let's just focus on a few of the basics. (see handouts that follow)

Guided Practice:

Students will take out the paragraph they began revising the day before. It has already been recopied and double spaced. They should now focus on simple revision strategies – inserting prepositional phrases, adverbs, adverb clauses, participial phrases, and appositives to enhance fluency. Remind students to pay particular attention to sentence beginnings.

Conclusion:

The main purpose for varying sentence patterns is to ensure that your writing does not sound like a list. This can be accomplished by using different kinds of sentences as well as different lengths of sentences. During revision of sentence structure, focus on simple strategies, paying particular attention to sentence beginnings.

Assessment:

Check over group paragraphs or have students partner up with another group and share.

Reflection:

Using Clauses and Phrases to Create Sentence Variety

CLAUSE	**Every clause has a subject and a verb. A clause is either dependent or independent.**

Independent Clauses can stand alone.
They are also known as main clauses or insubordinate clauses.

Examples: *We went to the store* because we needed milk.
Before he eats breakfast, *John delivers papers.*

Dependent Clauses (also called subordinate clauses) cannot stand alone. They must be linked to an independent clause. There are three types of dependent clauses:

noun clause	Example:	They ate *whatever their mother fed them.*
adjective clause	Example:	Ryan was the one *who wanted cake.*
adverb clause	Example:	*After David devoured his second burger*, he decided he'd had enough.

An introductory dependent clause usually starts with: after, although, as, because, before, if, since, until, whenever, where, unless, whether, while, or wherever.

PHRASE	**A phrase does not contain a subject / verb. It is a single part of speech.**

There are six types of phrases:

prepositional phrase	begins with a preposition and ends with a noun or pronoun Example: under the table
adjective phrase	prepositional phrase that modifies a noun or pronoun Example: She ate her ham sandwich with mustard.
adverb phrase	prepositional phrase that modifies a verb, an adjective, or another adverb Example: She always eats in her office.
participial phrase	verb form that can be used as an adjective Example: Finishing the pie, she got up.
gerund phrase	verb form ending in *ing* that is used as a noun Example: Eating is important.
infinitive phrase	verb form, usually preceded by *to* Example: It is time to eat.

EASY Strategies for Creating Varied Sentence Patterns

The purpose for varying sentence patterns is to maintain interest and create fluency in writing. Unfortunately, once all the options have names, many students are confused and overwhelmed. They avoid revision strategies related to sentence structure because of the vast number of choices there are. Here are a few basic strategies that are easily remembered and understood.

1) Begin a sentence with a prepositional phrase.

A prepositional phrase serves as an adjective or adverb. It consists of a preposition, its object, and any words that modify the object.

Examples: *After the game* we ate dinner.
Around the corner was our favorite restaurant, so we ate dinner
During the meeting we ate dinner.

The Most Common Prepositions:

about	before	except	on	until
above	behind	for	out	up
across	below	from	outside	upon
after	beneath	in	over	with
against	beside	inside	since	
along	between	into	through	
among	beyond	like	till	
around	by	near	to	
as	down	of	toward	
at	during	off	under	

Consider using these prepositional phrases for paragraph transitions:

After a while	Before we knew it	During the night
Against all odd	Behind the scenes	In the meantime
At the end of the day	Beyond a shadow of a doubt	Up until that time

Prepositional phrases can also be used to combine short sentences.

The chocolate chip cookies smelled so good. They were still in the oven.
The chocolate chip cookies in the oven smelled so good.

2) **Begin a sentence with an adverb (or adverb clause).**

Adverbs modify or describe a verb, an adjective or another adverb.

Examples: *Yesterday* we drove to Joe's Diner for lunch.
Finally, we found a place that sold pancakes.
Later we felt sick to our stomachs.
Obviously, we won't return to that restaurant.

Adverbs can also be used to combine or enhance sentence quality.

Examples: We were *extremely* hungry when we arrived, so we ordered *as soon as* we sat *down.*

It was *awfully* smoky, so we decided to eat as *quickly* as possible.
The server was *actually* pleasant, and we tipped her *well.*

Adverb clauses are subordinate clauses that modify verbs, adjectives, or adverbs. They tell how, when, where, why, or what.

Examples: *Although I know I shouldn't*, I will eat a double cheeseburger.
After the meal is over, we will start thinking about dessert.
Whenever we come to this restaurant, I gain weight.

Common Words that Introduce Adverb Clauses

after
although
as
as if
as soon as
as though
because

unless whenever
until while
when
where
wherever
before
so that

Adverb Clauses can also be used to combine short, related sentences.

Examples: We decided to eat *because we were hungry.*
You're eating *as though you haven't seen food* in a week.
We can all split a pizza, *unless something else sounds better.*

3) Include a participial phrase, especially at the beginning of the sentence.

A participial phrase is a group of words that consists of a participle and its object. Participles are either present (ending in ing) or past (ending in ed). They are verb forms that are used as adjectives.

Examples: *Realizing* we were hungry, we pulled into the nearest restaurant.
Choosing this restaurant wasn't my idea, but I went with the majority.
Noticing there wasn't a crowd should have been a clue of what was to come.

Participles can also be used to enhance meaning.

Examples: I had a *sinking f*eeling that they wouldn't have anything I wanted.
The *battered* menu looked like it had seen better days.
The *overcooked* burgers were like hockey pucks.

4) Use appositives to combine short sentences and enhance meaning.

An appositive is a noun or pronoun that explains or identifies another noun.

Examples: Joe's Diner, *our most popular restaurant*, is around the corner.
The Italian food, *especially the lasagna*, is a popular choice.
The Friday night special, *fish and chips*, brings in the crowds.

Remember: Rather than overloading with all the choices available for varying sentence patterns, start with a few that are familiar. The purpose is to create interest and to enhance fluency.

Remember to use all kinds of sentences (classified by structure and purpose).
Include prepositional phrases, especially at the beginning of a sentence.
Insert adverbs (or adverb clauses).
Use participial phrases, especially at the beginning of a sentence.
Include appositives to enhance clarity.
Always read over your work, concentrating on sentence fluency.

Week 6: Exceptional Supporting Details — Day 1

Title: ***Precise Verbs, Proper Nouns, Powerful Adjectives*** **Time: 60 minutes**

Behavioral Objectives: Students will:
- revise to improve supporting details

Academic Standards: Revise for meaning and clarity.
Use precise language and action verbs.

Materials Needed: Writing sample from Day 1

Introduction:

Student review of Simple 6™ components.

Let's take a look at your writing from Day 1.
Divide a blank sheet of paper into 3 columns. Label the columns:
PRECISE VERBS PROPER NOUNS ADJECTIVES

(Review verbs, nouns, and adjectives if necessary.) *Take about five minutes to read your Day 1 writing sample. List the words you used in each category.*

Lesson:

The purpose of today's lesson is to review strategies you can use for revision other than inserting adjectives. Precise verbs should create a clear image in the reader's mind. Proper nouns will give specific names to people, places, and events. Adjectives can usually be reduced in number and improved upon in quality.

Guided Practice:

Revise your Day 1 paper using precise verbs, proper nouns, and carefully-selected adjectives.

Conclusion:

Remember: Replacing overused verbs with more precise language; giving people, places, and things names, and inserting carefully-selected adjectives should be an automatic part of your revision strategy.

Assessment:

Look over revisions to see if corrections were made.

Reflection:

Week 6: Exceptional Supporting Details — Day 2

Title: ***Using Imagery or Other Literary Devices*** **Time: 60 minutes**

Behavioral Objectives: Students will:

- use various literary techniques to improve descriptive writing

Academic Standards: Use figurative language and other literary techniques to enhance clarity and artistic effect.
Use effective and interesting language.
Enhance meaning by using rhetorical devices.

Materials Needed: Handout on the next page
First day writing sample

Introduction:

Student review of Simple 6™ components.

Literary techniques are strategies that are used to make writing more descriptive. You have learned many over the years. Let's make a list, beginning with simile. What other literary techniques have you learned over the years?

Lesson:

If appropriate, give students a handout of the next page. Any of the literary techniques on the following page may be used as a lesson focus. Lessons taught should be determined by student need and by academic standards listed at that particular grade level.

Guided Practice:

Students will continue to revise their first-day writing, using at least three of the literary techniques discussed. Share before / after sentences with the group.

Conclusion:

Bring your reader "to the moment" by using literary techniques in your writing. Pay more attention to these techniques as they are used in literature.

Assessment:

Reflection:

A Short List of Literary Techniques

alliteration: *using two or more words together that start with the same sound.*

anecdote: *a brief account of an event used to make a point.*

colloquialism: *a common, everyday expression.*

exaggeration: *the act of stretching the truth.*

foreshadowing: *hints about what is going to happen.*

humor: *things that make the reader laugh.*

idiom: *expressions that mean something different from their literal context.*

imagery: *language used to appeal to the reader's senses.*

irony: *the use of a word or phrase to mean the opposite of its normal meaning.*

metaphor: *an implied comparison of two different things.*

onomatopoeia: *the use of a word that imitates a sound.*

oxymoron: *two contradictory words come together for special effect.*

personification: *human qualities given to animals or inanimate objects.*

persuasion: *writing that is meant to influence the reader's opinion.*

pun: *a play on words that suggests a different meaning.*

sarcasm: a *harsh or cutting type of humor.*

satire: *the use of irony, sarcasm, or ridicule to convey true meaning*

simile: *a comparison that uses like or as.*

Week 7: Audience/Voice — Day 1

Title: *Tone* — **Time: 60 minutes**

Behavioral Objectives: Students will:
- identify the tone of the writing sample.
- adjust the tone of their writing to fit the task.

Academic Standards: Develop unique style and voice.
Use tone for appropriate purposes.
Revise to improve tone.

Materials Needed: Examples of various tones of writing *(next page)*

Introduction:

What does it mean to "adjust the tone or style of the writing to fit the audience"? It's basically about attitude.

As you write, are you trying to convey an attitude that is: formal or informal
amusing or serious
sincere or satirical

Lesson:

Share short excerpts of student writing, identifying formal, informal, amusing, serious, sincere, and satirical writing styles. Discuss the importance of appropriateness for the task. What is your purpose for writing? Is it to inform, to persuade, or to entertain? Think of the purpose for writing when deciding on the tone that will be used.

Guided Practice:

Read the paragraphs on the following page. In a large group setting or working in small groups, discuss the tone of each and determine whether or not it was appropriate for the task or audience.

Conclusion:

Always think of the purpose for writing when determining the tone that will be used.

Assessment:

Reflection:

Writing Samples: *Identify the Tone*

Student Sample 1: **TONE: ______________________ APPROPRIATE? _____**

The responsibilities of the average producer are immeasurable in the music environment. Today's music and movie producers perform thousands of tasks daily. Obviously, the stress level of having this job is tremendously high, with stress coming from every direction. Whether it's meeting a deadline, discussing creative differences, writing lyrics, coaching vocals, or overseeing the recording session, this is definitely a high-stress position. In considering a career as a music producer, consider all the multi-tasking that is required, and be expecting a huge amount of stress!

Student Sample 2: **TONE: ______________________ APPROPRIATE? _____**

I have come to a point in my life where I feel that I deserve an allowance for the many duties I do each week. Before you say no, I request your attention while I present my reasons.

I will not whine, "But all my friends get an allowance!" No. I think I should have an allowance because it will keep me from annoying you with, "Can I have some money?" (Although I suppose there is a slight chance that you will hear me asking for my allowance.)

With an allowance, I'll learn to be much more responsible. Besides, I presently feel overworked and underpaid. I am quite sure you are curious about how much it will be. Am I correct? Do not fret, for I have a plan. . .

Student Sample 3: **TONE: ______________________ APPROPRIATE? _____**

Gazing out my window, everything appears peaceful and quiet. I am beckoned outside where the leaves lightly nip my ankles in the breeze. Birds chirp quietly as the sun is drawn to the horizon. The colorful hues of the sky, clinging to their vibrancy, are soft and slow to change. The dead leaves in the trees dance slowly, alone. The mere simplicity of it all mesmerizes me. As the stars slowly pierce the night sky I wonder, will there ever be another time just like this?

Week 7: Audience/Voice — Day 2

Title: ***Voice*** **Time: 60 minutes**

Behavioral Objectives: Students will:
- use strategies to make a personal connection with the audience.

Academic Standards: Develop unique style and voice.
Revise to highlight voice.

Materials Needed: literature selections with exceptional voice
newspaper articles (*various types*)
student writing samples (*provided*)

Introduction:

Voice is nothing more than how your words sound on the page. It's all about personality and whether the reader feels a personal connection to the writer. Whether the purpose for writing is to persuade, to inform, or to entertain, the writer's honesty and passion should come through. You are trying to make the reader care about what is being said.

Lesson:

Some pointers for incorporating voice into your writing:

Be honest. If you believe it, your audience is more likely to.
Think of your audience. If you are trying to connect with them, who are they?
Share your feelings as descriptively as you can.
State your opinions with conviction and passion.
Just be yourself. If you write the way you speak, it should "sound" like you.

Share selections from recent in-class reading that show exceptional voice (*and/or use examples on the next page).*

Guided Practice:

Free Write: *Take ten minutes to write about a time that you were very excited about something. Try to bring your audience to the moment. Tell it like it really was. . . Does it "sound" like you?*

OR Revise the second student sample that is provided. Include voice.

Collect papers. As the teacher reads them orally, can students identify the writer?

Conclusion:

Use voice to make your writing your own. Think of your audience, because the purpose is to connect with them. Don't stress over it; just be yourself.

Assessment:

Student revisions will include voice, making a direct connection with the audience.

Reflection:

Using Voice in your Writing to Connect with the Audience

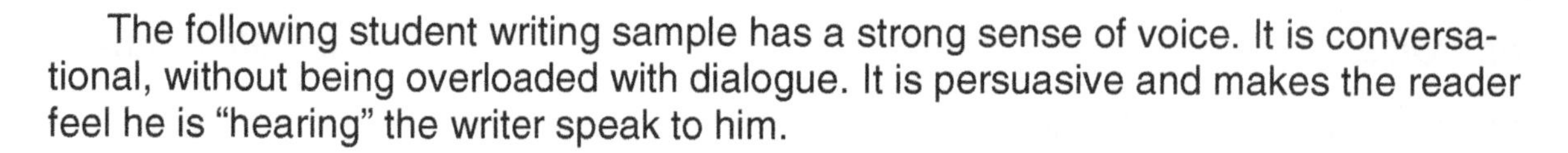

The following student writing sample has a strong sense of voice. It is conversational, without being overloaded with dialogue. It is persuasive and makes the reader feel he is "hearing" the writer speak to him.

Writing Task: Your friend has just gotten the answers to tomorrow's math test and is willing to give them to you. Will you cheat?

Student Writing Sample: **Cheating**

Cheat? You want me to cheat???!!! Cheating is wrong! Cheating is a sin! While I was growing up if I ever cheated I would get spanked, and then I'd get a long lecture on top of it! Now that I am old enough to really understand the consequences, I can tell you this - I am responsible enough to say, "No Thanks!!"

Cheating can get you in HUGE trouble if you get caught, but it could also get you in trouble if you don't get caught. Look at it this way. If you cheat, you will not learn anything. If you cheat off someone who has the answers wrong, it doesn't take a rocket scientist to put two and two together.

If you do get caught, the consequences are not pretty. The best (and most unlikely) thing that could happen to you is you take the test over alone. More likely though, your parents are going to get called at work. While you listen, you'll be praying that the principal doesn't say he's calling to let them know you've been suspended. So ask yourself this. Is it REALLY worth it? No way!! Nobody will ever get me to cheat.

This student writing sample lacks voice. There is little or no connection to the audience. Think about how this piece might be revised to make a direct impact on the audience.

Writing Task: Write an essay that describes how you and your family feel about homework.

Student Writing Sample: **Homework**

Homework is important to my mom and dad, but I don't really care for homework. The reason is homework isn't important to me at all. I don't enjoy doing homework, because it takes half of my day away. It's boring and I hate it. I do my homework and I get it in on time.

The thing that distracts me the most is TV. I do my homework in front of the TV and do the work at the commercials. It is sometimes hard to do it a few minutes at a time, but that is the method I use. Another thing that distracts me is my brother. He is always bugging me by talking, singing, or doing some other annoying behavior. It all keeps me from doing something I didn't want to do in the first place.

Homework is valued in my family, but not by me.

Your comments:

Week 8: Scoring — Day 1

Title: ***Practice and Discussion*** **Time: 60 minutes**

Behavioral Objectives: Students will:

- evaluate pieces of writing
- score writing samples using
- The Simple 6™mini rubric

Academic Standards: Review and evaluate written work.
Provide constructive criticism to other writers.

Materials Needed: student writing samples *(on the next page or your own)*
mini rubric

Introduction:

Give each student The Simple 6™ mini rubric. Explain how to use it. Remind students that the topic point won't be given until they get into the piece, the logical order point will probably be last due to the conclusion, and other points will be given as "evidence of mastery" is shown at least three times in the writing. Tally marks should be placed to the right of each component before giving the final point.

Lesson:

Score student writing samples. Model the first sample for the whole class, using a mini rubric. (If they are not available, the components have been listed at the bottom of each sample. Circle or put a 1 underneath those that get points.) Do the second sample together. Answer any questions students have. Entertain discussion and respectful argument.

We can try to simplify the scoring of student writing, but it will never be easy. We will sometimes not agree. Always make sure you can justify your points; the score should never be a guess.

Guided Practice:

Have students score the other samples alone or in a group of two or three.
Discuss scores given and rationale for points.

Conclusion:

Students should now understand how points are given, the order of thinking through the scoring, and how there may sometimes be discussion and non agreement between scorers.

Assessment:

Tally scores given by each group. Meet with groups whose scores vary by more than one point from the rest of the class.

Reflection:

Name ______________________ **Writing Sample**
Teacher ______________________ **Secondary GR** ___
Date ______________________ **SCORE:**

Is Honesty the Best Policy?

Read the writing prompt below and complete the writing activity.

Several students in your class have been cheating. They have been copying one another's homework assignments, getting research papers off the Internet, and stealing copies of final exams. You think it's wrong, and you are glad that you haven't been involved.

Last night you got a phone call from a close friend. He has the answers to tomorrow's math test. He knows you are not doing too well in this class and will probably be grounded if your grade does not improve.

Write a descriptive essay explaining what you will do. Tell why you made the decision and how you feel about cheating in this particular instance.

Be sure to:

plan your writing before you begin.
include an introduction, a body, and a strong conclusion.
focus on the following ideas:
a clear statement of your decision
your feelings about why you made this choice
include exceptional supporting details to make your essay interesting.

Your writing will not be scored on your personal opinions. It will be scored objectively on:

- *how clearly you address the prompt*
- *how well you organize your ideas*
- *how effectively you express yourself*
- *how consistently you use correct paragraphing, grammar, spelling, and punctuation.*

Be sure to use the Standard Rules of English, which do not include slang or jargon.

Week 8

Writing Task: *Is Honesty the Best Policy?*

Student Sample #1 **Score: _____**

If someone told me that they had the answers to a Math test and offered them to me I would never accept them because I wouldn't feel right about cheating. I don't like to cheat and I could get caught!

Instead, I would study long and hard. I would study all night until the test and even ask my parents for help.

The day of the test I will go and tell the teacher that some kids have the answers and hope she would change the test. If she did, who ever had the answers would get everything wrong. If she did not, I would still get a good grade while the other person would have to feel guilty for the rest of his life.

I would rather get a B by studying than an A+ from cheating even if I did not get grounded.

TOPIC **ORDER** **VOCABULARY** **PATTERNS** **DETAILS** **AUDIENCE**

Writing Task: *Is Honesty the Best Policy?*

Student Sample #2 **Score:** _____

I would say no. I would also tell him that he should not be cheating and not to call me if he is going to be giving me the answers on assignments or tests. I would feel like I should still be friends with them, but they shouldn't try to give me answers again. I would also study REALLY hard that night for the test, and maybe ask that friend if they would like to study together. Also if during a test someone tried to cheat off my test, I would use a cover-up sheet.

The End

TOPIC **ORDER** **VOCABULARY** **PATTERNS** **DETAILS** **AUDIENCE**

Writing Task: *Is Honesty the Best Policy?*

Student Sample #3 **Score:** _____

I would never accept the answers to a test because of the consequential effects that would certainly follow. First off, cheating is dishonest! Getting a reputation for being dishonest can dramatically change your life! It can ruin your chances of getting outstanding recommendations for a job or a scholarship. Why would you consciously jeopardize the way others judge your character? There are emotional side effects too. You'll have to deal with the guilt, you'll be inclined to cheat again, and you'll constantly be looking over your shoulder thinking you'll get caught. If you think any of those options are acceptable, think again!

Spiderman's uncle once said, "With great power, comes great responsibilities." There are choices to be made here. First, I could get away with it, but I know I would feel guilty. Second, I could get caught, and then I'd be in major trouble. The third choice, my preference, is to just not cheat and get on with my life. Sure, I could get a lousy grade on the test, but I'll gladly take those consequences and still be able to sleep at night.

I have to believe that most students would not cheat because of the guilt, the consequences that come with getting caught, and the simple fact that cheating is not honorable. So if you are put in this situation, think about what I've said here. It's never worth it to cheat!

TOPIC **ORDER** **VOCABULARY** **PATTERNS** **DETAILS** **AUDIENCE**

Writing Task: *Is Honesty the Best Policy?*

Student Sample #4 **Score:** _____

Get this, my friend called me last night. He had the answers to the math test. I was shocked! I didn't know how to react at first. Then I came to my senses.

My answer is no to cheating. I would never cheat because it is wrong. It is wrong because it is not the truth or a solution to learning. My church and my parents have taught me to be honest. Also, if I cheated I would fail the test if I got caught.

When my friend called, I told him that I am not going to cheat. I will study for the test and take pride in my work. I would not learn the math by cheating. It would lead to failing a final exam. I would tell my teacher that some students are cheating.

I feel that my friend should not cheat and try to get me to cheat with him. I feel that I should not hang around with this friend anymore. I am an honest person. I feel bad telling on my classmates, but it is the right thing to do. I know if I study hard enough I can get a good grade on the test.

As it turned out I passed the class. I didn't get grounded or in trouble. On the other hand some of my classmates did fail the class. They made the wrong choice. Maybe next time my friend will listen to me.

TOPIC **ORDER** **VOCABULARY** **PATTERNS** **DETAILS** **AUDIENCE**

Week 8

Writing Task: *Is Honesty the Best Policy?*

Student Sample # 5 **Score: _____**

Are you kidding? Yes I would cheat if I was failing! But I wouldn't help steal it, I would just copy it. I would also miss a few so it wouldn't look like I cheated, so it looked like I studied. I wouldn't feel that bad about it because there are a lot worse things that could have happened. Don't you agree with me?

TOPIC **ORDER** **VOCABULARY** **PATTERNS** **DETAILS** **AUDIENCE**

Writing Task: *Is Honesty the Best Policy?*

Student Sample #6 **Score:** _____

If my friend called and asked me if I wanted the answers to our math test tomorrow, I would tell her thanks, but no thanks. I think that cheating gets you no where in life. If you don't work hard and put effort in your work you will not get very far in life.

It would be tempting to get a good grade but I realize that it would be very momentary and then on the next test my grade would reflect my "normal" ability.

If I were to cheat I could not live with myself that I cheated on my math test. Even though the whole class may be getting an "A" on the test, I would still feel good about myself even if I did not get a great grade on the test.

I would be disappointed that some of my friends would say yes and take the answers to the test and tell everyone that they did all the work.

Besides cheating, I could not stand lying to my parents and teacher. The worst part about lying is that one lie leads to another and you almost always get caught.

I am sure I would feel some pressure from my friends that are cheating; but living with my decision would definitely be easier than living with lying and cheating and possibly getting in serious trouble.

TOPIC **ORDER** **VOCABULARY** **PATTERNS** **DETAILS** **AUDIENCE**

Suggested Scores for: *Is Honesty the Best Policy?*

Student Sample #1 **Score 2**

Analysis: *This paper focuses on the* ***topic*** *but has no conclusion, so no point is given for logical order. Vocabulary is basic.* ***Sentence patterns*** *create fluency and details are given, although not to the extent that they would be exceptional. Paragraphs are not developed. There is no connection with the audience.*

Student Sample #2 **Score 2**

Analysis: *This paper focuses on the* ***topic*** *and* ***attempts*** *to provide* ***details****. Nothing else is evident.*

Student Sample #3 **Score 6**

Analysis: *This paper focuses on the* ***topic*** *and has* ***logical order****.* ***Vocabulary words*** *such as consequential, dramatically, inclined, and preference are recognized.* ***Sentence patterns*** *contribute to fluency,* ***details*** *support the topic, and an* ***audience*** *connection is made.*

Student Sample #4 **Score 4**

Analysis: *This paper focuses on the* ***topic*** *and has* ***logical order****. Vocabulary is basic. Sentence patterns do not create fluency.* ***Details*** *are provided and a satisfactory* ***connection*** *is made with the audience.*

Student Sample #5 **Score 2**

Analysis: *Because of the length of this paper, it only receives points for focusing on the* ***topic*** *and making a connection with the* ***audience****. There are not enough details to carry that point.*

Student Sample #6 **Score 4**

Analysis: *This paper focuses on the* ***topic*** *and has* ***logical order****. Other than momentary, vocabulary is basic.* ***Sentence patterns*** *contribute to the fluency of the piece, but because so many paragraphs have been started but not developed, there is no point for supporting details. An* ***audience*** *connection is made.*

Week 8: Scoring — Day 2

Title: ***Practice and Discussion*** **Time: 60 minutes**

Behavioral Objectives: Students will:
- score student writing samples using The Simple 6™ rubric
- discuss their reasons for the score

Academic Standards: Review and evaluate written work.
Provide constructive criticism to other writers.

Materials Needed: prompt and student samples (on next pages)
mini rubrics (p. 81)

Introduction:

Yesterday we scored some actual student writing samples. Are there any questions? How many of you thought it was helpful to look at a piece of writing from the scorer's point of view? Hopefully, this will carry over as you do your own writing.

Lesson:

Let's review the components again quickly. This will reinforce what you are looking for as you score again today. Remember, you are looking for at least three pieces of "evidence of mastery" before assigning the final point.

Guided Practice:

Work in small groups to score six (or less) samples of the same prompt. Tally scores to see if there is overall agreement. Answer questions. Encourage discussion.

Conclusion:

Answer any additional questions students may have.

Assessment:

Check for general agreement on the score points as students work in small groups or during whole group discussion.

Reflection:

Name ____________________ **Writing Sample**
Teacher____________________ **Secondary GR** ___
Date ____________________ **SCORE:**

Where's Your Homework?

Read the information in the box. Then do the writing activity.

More and more students come to school each day without their homework. Watching too much TV, working late hours in a part-time job, caring for younger siblings, chatting on-line, or phoning/text messaging are all possible reasons for students not doing their homework.

Write an essay that tells how you and your parents feel about homework. Is homework important in your family? Do other things get in the way of homework? Are you one of those students who always completes homework on time or not? Does your situation need improvement?

Prewriting Activity:

Plan your writing before you begin.
Include an inviting introduction, an organized body, and a strong conclusion.
Focus on the following ideas:
Is homework valued in your family?
Do you complete your homework or not?
What things keep you from doing your homework?
Does your situation need improvement?
Include specific details and examples to make your writing interesting and descriptive.

Your writing will not be scored on your personal opinions. It will be scored objectively on:

- *how clearly you address the prompt*
- *how well you organize your ideas*
- *how effectively you express yourself*
- *how consistently you use correct paragraphing, grammar, spelling, and punctuation.*

Be sure to use the Standard Rules of English, which do not include slang or jargon.

Writing Task: *Where's Your Homework?*

Student Sample #1 **Score:** _____

I don't really care about homework unless I'm in a school sport, then I really try to do my best. My mom and dad really like good grades on assignments and if I don't do really good they might get mad, and sometimes not get mad it depends on how they feel or what subject it is in. So homework is not really important, but sometimes it is.

Sometimes, like if my friends call me I'm going to talk to them first, or like a sport might go for awhile so I can't do my homework for awhile. I mostly get my homework done on time but sometimes I don't. I think it's okay to get a bad grade once in a while but not a lot of bad grades. Mabe, but I think I'm good where I'm at right now but mabe later in life.

TOPIC **ORDER** **VOCABULARY** **PATTERNS** **DETAILS** **AUDIENCE**

Week 8

Writing Task: *Where's Your Homework?*

Student Sample #2 **Score: _____**

To my family and I homework is very important. As soon as I get home from practice I do my homework. It's valued to me because I want to get into the University of Notre Dame, and get a great job paying big money. For my parents they always want to see me succeed. They want me to have a great job, and to see me going to any University I want. So they push me to get good grades.

I always complete my homework assignments. I take pride in finishing my homework. I think everybody should feel that way.

TOPIC **ORDER** **VOCABULARY** **PATTERNS** **DETAILS** **AUDIENCE**

Writing Task: *Where's Your Homework?*

Student Sample #3 **Score:** _____

Homework is usually the top priority in my house. It is the key to being able to hang out after school or sports practice. Homework is well-valued in my family. My grades can NEVER fall under a C- or I'm in a huge helping of trouble. Every once in a while though my grades may slip and I'll have to suffer the consequences, and believe me, they aren't very pretty.

I normally get my homework done in time for class or I'll get it done the day before. If I don't get my homework done in time it's usually because I left it at school, or maybe I had soccer practice and forgot to do it,. Normally though, I get it done. My forgetfulness needs a little bit of improvement but for the most part I'm doing pretty well on getting it done on time.

This school year I would like to be more organized. Last year I definitely think my homework needed to be more organized. When I went to go and find something in my locker everything was all mixed up and crinkled. Since a lot of it was so crinkled I couldn't tell which assignment was which, I would just grab one and hope it was the correct one to turn in. Sometimes I was lucky, and other times I wasn't.

This year so far I've been neater and a lot more organized and so far it's working. Also, the teachers give us more time in class to work on homework.

TOPIC ORDER VOCABULARY PATTERNS DETAILS AUDIENCE

Writing Task: *Where's Your Homework?*

Student Sample #4 **Score:** ____

In my family somebody just asks did you get your homework done, without really caring. Homework you get a lot of it so it adds up. If you don't do it you could get really bad grades. I'm gonna try to get my homework this year.

TOPIC **ORDER** **VOCABULARY** **PATTERNS** **DETAILS** **AUDIENCE**

Week 8

Writing Task: *Where's Your Homework?*

Student Sample #5 **Score:** _____

I feel like homework is a good way to review the materials that we learned that day in class. Homework also helps to get us prepared for a class test. But I think my family and I believe we get too much homework.

After a while, homework starts to feel like a chore, and it isn't fun or easy to complete. Homework isn't always easy to get done. Our family has other things that get in the way like Wednesday night church, sport practices, youth group, and errands that need to be done. I usually always get my homework done, but sometimes I don't. I skip questions because I don't understand the materials or I can't remember the instructions.

I think if I would make a commitment to getting my homework done right after school it would be easier. And if I would concentrate and take my time, I would improve in my grades.

TOPIC **ORDER** **VOCABULARY** **PATTERNS** **DETAILS** **AUDIENCE**

Writing Task: *Where's Your Homework?*

Student Sample #6 **Score:** _____

Both of my parents are high school teachers. Almost every day, they come home and complain to each other about a class or student that was exceptionally annoying or just plain apathetic. Because of this, homework has always been an important focus during my after-school hours.

It's sometimes difficult for me to complete my homework, especially in the spring and fall when I play soccer. It takes up a lot of my time, especially when I have a coach that likes to have long, frequent practices. By the time I get home, I'm exhausted! All I want to do is take a long shower and relax. Homework isn't exactly enjoyable when you're tired.

Because those two things take up so much time, that poses another problem for me. I love to watch TV. I am absolutely addicted to CSI, and I watch almost every crime drama available on TV. I admit, I will almost always watch a new episode of CSI before I do my homework; still, I get it done.

It may sound like I'm complaining, but I'm really not. Most of the time, it's not an insurmountable problem. I generally don't mind staying up a little late to finish an assignment. We usually don't get too much (and most all of it is easy). Homework, like it or not, is always going to be part of school. It's important because your grades determine your immediate future, especially in terms of college choice. I most definitely want to attend college, and by doing my homework I'm ensuring that I'll make more than minimum wage when I become an adult.

TOPIC **ORDER** **VOCABULARY** **PATTERNS** **DETAILS** **AUDIENCE**

Suggested Scores for: *Where's Your Homework?*

Student Sample #1 **Score 2**

Analysis: *This paper focuses on the* ***topic.*** *Because there is no conclusion, and paragraphs are not structured according to the prompt, no point is given for logical order. Vocabulary is basic. Sentence patterns have structural problems. Details are given, although not to the extent that they would be exceptional. There is a connection with the* ***audience****. This would be a Score 2 or 3, depending on how you feel about the details.*

Student Sample #2 **Score 2**

Analysis: *This paper focuses on the* ***topic*** *and has basic* ***order****. There are not enough details, even for an attempt point.*

Student Sample #3 **Score 4**

Analysis: *This paper focuses on the* ***topic*** *and but misses the logical order point due to the lack of a conclusion. Vocabulary words are not challenging.* ***Sentence patterns*** *contribute to fluency,* ***details*** *support the topic, and an* ***audience*** *connection is made.*

Student Sample #4 **Score 1**

Analysis: *This paper* ***attempts*** *to* ***focus*** *on the topic.*

Student Sample #5 **Score 3**

Analysis: *This paper focuses on the* ***topic*** *and has* ***logical order****. Vocabulary is basic and many sentences start with I, eliminating the possibility of varied sentence patterns. Examples have been provided, but they haven't been developed in paragraphs. A connection has been made with the* ***audience.***

Student Sample #6 **Score 5**

Analysis: *This paper focuses on the* ***topic*** *and has* ***logical order. Vocabulary*** *words such as exceptionally annoying, poses, insurmountable, and ensuring were recognized as challenging.* ***Sentence patterns*** *contribute to the fluency of the piece. Details are supportive of the topic but could have been more indepth. An* ***audience*** *connection is made.*

The Simple 6™

0 / 1

___ Focus on the Topic
___ Logical Order
___ Challenging Vocabulary
___ Varied Sentence Patterns
___ Exceptional Supporting Details
___ Audience

___ TOTAL POINTS

Kay Davidson, Revised 2002

The Simple 6™

0 / 1

___ Focus on the Topic
___ Logical Order
___ Challenging Vocabulary
___ Varied Sentence Patterns
___ Exceptional Supporting Details
___ Audience

___ TOTAL POINTS

Kay Davidson, Revised 2002

The Simple 6™

0 / 1

___ Focus on the Topic
___ Logical Order
___ Challenging Vocabulary
___ Varied Sentence Patterns
___ Exceptional Supporting Details
___ Audience

___ TOTAL POINTS

Kay Davidson, Revised 2002

The Simple 6™

0 / 1

___ Focus on the Topic
___ Logical Order
___ Challenging Vocabulary
___ Varied Sentence Patterns
___ Exceptional Supporting Details
___ Audience

___ TOTAL POINTS

Kay Davidson, Revised 2002

SCORING AT THE SECONDARY LEVEL

Grade 6-10: Planning and prewriting are essential. Questions within the prompt must be addressed. (If there are no questions, students must design their own.) Examples and exceptional details must support each topic sentence. Sentences should be more complex, and transitions should be smooth. There should be evidence of literary techniques that promote a personal connection with the audience.

SUGGESTED PROCEDURES:

Get a block of time (about an hour) in which you will score all papers.
Gather mini rubrics and a class analysis chart.
Score each paper, one at a time – without dwelling for long periods of time making decisions.

- Read it first. Assign the score based on only the components done well.
- OR: Decide if you think it is passing or not. Then assign points accordingly.

If you know it will not pass:

Decide which 3 components or less will get points.
Score 3 papers usually have length but many problems within.
Score 2 papers are short, weak attempts at completing the task. Many times these papers will be hard to read because of spelling and punctuation errors as well. "Attempt points" may be given.
Score 1 papers are *any* attempt at the task – even less than one sentence. Note *attempted* on the rubric for very weak papers.

If you know it is going to pass:

The stakes for each point get higher as you move toward the Score 6.

In **FOCUSING ON THE TOPIC,** prompt questions should be addressed.
How well did the writer accomplish the task?
LOGICAL ORDER must include a beginning, a middle, and an end.
Is the piece *introduced* with an inviting beginning or topic sentence?
Has the body been developed around the prompt questions?
Are transitions smooth? Is there a definite conclusion?
VOCABULARY should be precise and/or above grade level.
Have challenging vocabulary words or words specific to the subject been used?
Were the exceptional vocabulary words used correctly?
If **VARIED SENTENCE PATTERNS** were used, did they contribute to the fluency of the piece?
Do you see evidence of complex sentence structure?
There should be many EXCEPTIONAL SUPPORTING **DETAILS**.
Are examples given that are supported by additional details?
Were specific literary techniques used?
Did the writer appeal to your senses?
Was a strong attempt made to create a visual image?
Writer should have definitely connected with the **AUDIENCE**.
Do tone, enthusiasm, compassion, humor, personal style, or other literary devices pull you into the writing?

Transferring Rubric Scores to Percentages for a Grade

Score 6: Content Rubric		
6	97-100	A+
5	90-96	A
4	80-89	B
3	70-79	C
2	60-69	D
1	below 59	F

Scoring Content

Suppose a student writing sample has received a rubric score of 5 on content. Look at the line for a Score 5. It falls into the 90-96% category. (If this is not your grading scale, adjust the numbers accordingly.) While the content is fresh in your mind, ask yourself, "Is it closer to a Score 4 or a Score 6?" If it is closer to a Score 4, assign a percentage score closer to 90%. If it is closer to a Score 6, give a score closer to 96%.

Scoring Conventions

The conventions score has many different considerations, depending on the state. Some states give just one writing score, which includes conventions. Others evaluate conventions as either being mostly right or mostly wrong. Did the number of errors impact the reader's fluency? Still other states have a separate rubric for conventions, which may or may not have the same total number of points as the content rubric.

For grade book purposes, consider avoiding rubric scores for language usage, or conventions. Conventions are isolated grammar and usage skills that are being put into use, either correctly or incorrectly. The evaluation of conventions does not resemble the subjective nature of evaluating content. Therefore, I recommend taking a certain number of points off of 100% for each error. My personal preference is three points per error. Giving a concrete percentage score rather than a general rubric score gives teachers a much clearer indication of those students who need individual assistance and remediation.

Week 9: Revision — Day 1

Title: ***Attack it! Simple 6™ it!*** **Time: 60 minutes**

Behavioral Objectives: Students will:

- review The Simple 6™ Advanced Checklist
- practice revision strategies

Academic Standards:
Review and evaluate written work.
Revise, edit, and proofread.
Revise for meaning, clarity, and content.
Revise to highlight voice and sentence variety.
Revise to improve logic, coherence, and word choice.

Materials Needed: Advanced Simple 6™ Checklist (Chapter 5)

Introduction:

Give students a copy of the Basic Reminders for Revision (on the following page) for their writing notebook. Review revision strategies.

Lesson:

Model revision steps with a writing sample on the overhead. Follow the steps in the handout.

Guided Practice:

Students will work in small groups to practice revision strategies.

Conclusion:

If you follow a simple revision procedure, you're more likely to cover all the bases, especially if you are writing to an on-demand prompt that must be completed in a specific amount of time. Make sure to keep the revision strategies in a writing notebook.

Assessment:

Informal observation during group work and discussion OR collect revised papers from each group and peruse or grade.

Reflection:

Basic Steps for Revision

First, read the piece carefully!

Attack it!

Does it focus on the topic, answering all the questions in the prompt?

Is there and introduction, body and conclusion?

Simple 6™ it!

Find *at least* three overused or low-level words that could be more challenging.

Check sentence patterns. Is your writing fluent?

Use the four basic strategies for creating descriptive sentences.

1. Insert precise verbs.
2. Identify people, places, and things with proper nouns.
3. Insert powerful, carefully-selected adjectives.
4. Use imagery or other literary devices to appeal to the reader's senses.

Beginning Revision Strategies

Whole Group Prompt

All students revise the same writing sample, which is usually a Score 2 or 3.

Students work together in groups of 4-5.

Each group has a copy of the same sample (on transparency if possible).

One student is the writer-reader.

Students are given 15 minutes to see if they can get the sample to a Score 6.

A second student leads the scoring and follow-up discussion as each group shares their revision.

Writing Task: *Is Honesty the Best Policy*

Student Sample for Revision: **Score ____**

There have been several students cheating in my class. Last night, my best friend called me up and told me he had the answers to tomorrow's math test. He said he would give them to me to help get my grade up so I don't get grounded when report cards come out. It was an easy decision to make.

I refused his offer but he still tried to coax me into cheating. After that phone conversation we didn't speak to each other again. I did not feel good about loosing my best friend but I was happy with my decision. I believe it was the right thing to do. When test day came around my used-to-be best friend got caught cheating. I got a B+ on the test that I took. He received a zero for his grade.

I think it's the worst thing you can do at school. If you cheat, you are not learning what you need to know to get a good life when you are older. My satisfaction comes from working hard and being honest. I feel happy that I overcame peer pressure, I also learned that if I am not doing well in school and getting bad grades, that I just need to work twice as hard as I did before.

Week 9: Revision — Day 2

Title: ***Practice and Discussion*** **Time: 60 minutes**

Behavioral Objectives: Students will:

- work with a partner to score and revise a writing sample to a Score 6

Academic Standards:
Review and evaluate written work.
Revise, edit, and proofread.
Revise for meaning, clarity, and content.
Revise to highlight voice and sentence variety.
Revise to improve logic, coherence, and word choice.

Materials Needed: any piece of writing that needs to be revised (on transparency)

Introduction:

What are the basic steps to revision? (Review.) Are there any questions?

Lesson:

As a class, score the writing sample together on the overhead.

Guided Practice:

Work with a partner for 20 minutes to revise this writing sample to a Score 6.

Conclusion:

Informally observe during work session. After 10-15 minutes ask if there is a group that thinks they have a Score 6. If so, have one group read its paper while the class scores. This can be done auditorily (and it's difficult!) OR students can make revisions on a transparency and share them with the class.

Assessment:

Grade papers that were revised by partners. (They will be hard to read unless you have one student copy it over. Consider giving them an extra day to recopy if class time is not available.)

Reflection:

Chapter Conclusion

Students now have an introduction to The Simple 6™. From here, they just need opportunities to practice what they have learned. That means writing regularly and for a variety of reasons. Keep revisiting weak areas every other week, encouraging students to become masters at revision. On the opposite weeks, engage in other kinds of writing. A nine-week schedule might look something like this:

First Grading Period

Implement The Simple 6™ writing program. It takes about two hours a week for nine weeks. It is possible to condense it into six weeks.

All Following Grading Periods

Weeks 2 4 6
Revisit weak areas with lessons and practice. Follow the two-day format if possible. Identify weaknesses from your completed Class Analysis Chart.

Week 8
Formal assessment. If this strategy is in place on the school improvement plan, it will be a school-wide or district-wide task. All grade levels will complete the same on-demand writing task. All teachers will be accountable, and data will be turn in.

Weeks 1 3 5 7 9
Engage students in other types of writing. This may include paragraph development, specific literary devices or techniques, focus in a certain genre, analysis and reflection of literature, or non-fiction, research-based writing. The choice belongs to the English teacher but is driven by the academic standards. The main idea is to keep students writing!

Now that students know The Simple 6™, the rest of the staff can begin their contribution to the school improvement goal. English teachers may feel that the "work is done", so what can content-area teachers possibly do? There are several strategies content-area teachers can put in place to make your school a place where writing is valued across the curriculum. The amount of time spent on writing and the type of tasks content-area teachers will do should ultimately be decided by the staff. Opting out, however, is not a viable option. While some teachers may be better writers than others, writing is a life-long skill that can be nurtured and improved with contributions from every teacher.

Chapter 4 provides choices and content-related tasks that will guide content area teachers through the writing improvement process.

Chapter 3 Assessment: The Prompts

Whether the assessment is local or standardized, a prompt is usually provided for assessment writing. Students are encouraged to write as much as they can, providing details based on the information given in the prompt. Prompts fall into three specific categories, and each state has its own preference. As you design or use the prompts that have been provided, be sure to use the format followed by your state. The three categories of prompts are:

Prompts with Questions

Prompts without Questions

Prompts based on a Theme or Broad Idea

Prompts with Questions

In terms of guiding structure, prompts with questions are the easiest. If students have been taught to analyze a prompt and use the information provided rather than be intimidated by it, a prompt with questions clearly tells the writer what is expected to be included in the essay.

Prompts with questions usually start with a scenario or situation. The scenario is followed by questions that guide the writing content. They specifically suggest what the student should address in the essay. The second paragraph usually begins with the instructions. What is the writing task? The task is followed by a reiteration of the questions, usually in sentence format.

At the end of the prompt there is sometimes a reminder box with pre-writing suggestions for students. It may include reminders to plan in advance, include an introduction, body, and conclusion, focus on the questions being provided, and to include exceptional supporting details. Some prompts also provide an editing checklist for students to refer to as they reread their papers.

The following pages provide examples of prompts for middle and high school students. Completed Prompt Attack organizers and student anchor papers have been included for the first middle school prompt. The anchor papers are followed by 19 more prompts with questions that can be used at the middle school level.

The next section provides a completed prompt, Prompt Attack, and student anchor papers for high school students. These anchor papers are also followed by 19 additional prompts with questions that may be used at the high school level.

Prompts with Questions for Formal Assessment: Middle School

Sample Prompt: Vice President for a Day

Student Anchor Papers: Student writing samples are included that show examples of papers that received various scores from 1-6. Analysis is included that explains why points were given.

Additional Prompts with Questions for Classroom Use

Title	Genre
The After School Job	Persuasive
Cheer Up!	Narrative
My Favorite TV Show	Persuasive
How to Buy the Best Pair of Jeans	Expository
The Mysterious Check	Narrative
Just Another Day	Expository
It's Party Time!	Descriptive
Open Mouth, Insert Food	Narrative
Equal Opportunities	Persuasive
The Lottery	Descriptive
The Time Capsule	Descriptive
Don't Miss This One!	Persuasive
Snow Day!!	Descriptive
My Best Friend	Descriptive
Peer Pressure	Expository
I'm So Stressed Out!	Descriptive
School Rules	Persuasive
What a Difference!	Persuasive
Come Join Us!	Persuasive

Included on the next four pages is a template for a quarterly assessment packet, designed as a four-page booklet. The first page will guide you in writing your own prompts.

Name ________________________________
Teacher________________________________
Date________________________________

Secondary
Writing Assessment

SCORE __/6
__/4

Title

Read the information in the box and do the writing activity. Use other paper to plan your writing.

Prompt scenario. Questions.

Instructions. Repeat questions in sentence format.

Be sure to include:

____

____

____

____

____

____

____

____

____

____

____

____

____

Prompts

The Simple 6™ **A Writing Rubric for Students**

CONTENT RUBRIC

Ask these questions:
0 / 1

___	FOCUS ON THE TOPIC:	Did you **focus on the topic**, or did you run away with some other idea?
___	LOGICAL ORDER:	Have you presented your thoughts in a **logical order** that included an inviting introduction, a strong conclusion, and smooth transition?
___	CHALLENGING VOCABULARY:	Have you overused **challenging vocabulary** to make descriptions rich and explanations detailed and precise?
___	VARIED SENTENCE PATTERNS:	Did you use **varied sentence patterns** to create fluency?
___	EXCEPTIONAL SUPPORTING DETAILS:	Have you included **exceptional supporting details** that address all the specific points of the prompt?
___	AUDIENCE:	Did you write for a specific **audience**? Were you original, lively, or authoritative?
___/ 6	TOTAL POINTS	How many did you answer "yes?"

☐ SCORE 4 EXCEPTIONAL language skills	☐ SCORE 3 GOOD language skills	☐ SCORE 2 MINIMAL language skills	☐ SCORE 1 POOR language skills
• There are few or no errors in: capitalization punctuation grammar/usage run-ons/sentence fragments paragraphing spelling	• There are some errors in: capitalization punctuation grammar/usage run-ons/sentence fragments paragraphing spelling	• There are many errors in: capitalization punctuation grammar/usage run-ons/sentence fragments paragraphing spelling	• There are many serious errors in: capitalization punctuation grammar/usage run-ons/sentence fragments paragraphing spelling

Name	______________________	**Writing Sample**
Teacher	______________________	**Middle School GR** ___
Date	______________________	**SCORE:**

Vice President for a Day

Read the writing prompt below and complete the writing activity.

The Vice President of the United States has a great deal of authority, power, and responsibility in the day-to-day workings of the government. Yet, the public always hears more about the President than the Vice President. If you were Vice President for a day, what might your responsibilities be? What would your day be like? What kinds of things do you do that make an impact on our country?

Write a narrative essay that describes what your responsibilities might be if you were Vice President of the United States. Be sure to include your daily routine and the types of things you do that impact our country.

Be sure to:

plan your writing before you begin.
include an introduction, a body, and a strong conclusion.
focus on the following ideas:
your responsibilities
your daily routine
things you do to make an impact
include descriptive details that make your writing interesting.

Your writing will not be scored on your personal opinions. It will be scored objectively on:

- *how clearly you address the prompt*
- *how well you organize your ideas*
- *how effectively you express yourself*
- *how consistently you use correct paragraphing, grammar, spelling, and punctuation.*

Be sure to use the Standard Rules of English, which do not include slang or jargon.

Writing Task: Vice President for a Day

High

As I struggled with buttoning up my over coat, I quickly thought about what was about to happen. "It's almost time," I said to myself after looking at my watch and realizing it was 12:48 p.m. I was currently standing in the Blue Room of the White House, and I had to be in the Rose Garden by 1:00 p.m. "I can't be late for what will hopefully be the best day of my life," I said out loud as I quickly made my way through the mansion.

I was suddenly overwhelmed by the huge crowd that has assembled and hoped they were here for me. I walked confidently up onto the stage and sat down next to Herrold Coapstick, my opponent. At precisely 1:00 the President rose from his seat and made his way to the podium. "As President of the United States, my purpose today is to announce the newly appointed Vice President. However, before I do that I would first like to tell you exactly what my lower man does. He (or she, I guess I should include) makes the decisions I am too busy to make. He gives me advice when I need it the most, and most importantly he makes sure he is prepared to be the President at any given moment. Therefore, without this person, I would not be able to rule properly and the world would be even more screwed up than it already is. So, in conclusion, my choice for Vice President is Sarah Jane Smith."

I quickly stood up in astonishment. It was official! As I started to approach the microphone to give the speech I had been preparing for the past three days, the President whispered, "No need for a speech. We need to talk now!"

Prompts

High cont.

"I'm sorry, Ladies and Gentlemen. I've just received word that the remainder of this ceremony has been postponed until 6:00 p.m. this evening. I will give my formal acceptance speech at that time.

I had absolutely no idea what was going on. "In my first ten seconds on the job, I already had to rush everyone off of the property like an action packed bomb was about to go off! What's happening that is so important?" I asked the President.

"Sorry," said the President, "but we don't let any of the newbies do or say anything in their first week without being prepped first. You'll be leaving for Cancun this afternoon with your assistant, who will fill you in on what to do and say in public."

"Oh," I said with excitement and also some apprehension. As I packed for the trip to Cancun, I couldn't help reflecting on the fact that my first day in office would be spent rubbing on sun tan lotion and drinking a tropical drink with a little paper umbrella in it. What would the public think if they knew?

Analysis: Score 6

This paper focuses on the ***topic****, has logical* ***order****, and uses challenging* ***vocabulary*** *words such as overwhelmed, assembled, remainder, apprehension.* ***Sentence patterns*** *contribute to the overall fluency,* ***descriptions*** *are precise, and the* ***audience*** *connection is made.*

Average

If I was vice president for the day I would definetly do some fun things. I would first walk around the white house and look at everything there; just as if I was taking a tour. I have never been inside the white house so this would be a fun experience. I also of course would go see the President since I've never meet him in person either.

After meeting the president and taking the tour of the white house, I would go to my office. I always thought it would be kind of neat to have my own office. I would have the big wooden desk with my name on it. Except it probably wouldn't be as big as the presidents since I'm just the vice president. So anyways I would go to my office and check it out. I would also make it a little more modern. I would paint it lime green and have a whole bunch of lamps in there. I would post up a lot of pictures of my friends and family on the wall. I would make it my own little space. It would be much better than the president's office.

After redoing my office I would make some phone calls. I would call my friends first and talk to them and tell them all about being vice president. Then I would make some important business calls to people. I really don't know who thought, since I am not up to date with politics. I'm sure that I have important work that needs to be done.

Then after my responsibilities and duties are done, I would throw a party! I would invite all my friends and family. I would want them to admire my important special job of being vice president. There would be karoke and a DJ at my party. And of course, there would be junk food. We would stay up all night, watch scary movies, and prank peoples houses.

Then finally it would be morning. We would all have to go home. It would be sad. I would have to clean up my office and take everything home.

Analysis: Score 3 *This paper focuses on the **topic** even though the writer does not clearly answer each of the specific questions in the prompt. There is logical **order**. Vocabulary is ordinary. Several types of sentences are used, but the majority of them start with I. Details are provided but are not as precise as one would expect from the prompt. The connection with the **audience** is satisfactory, given the level of writing.*

Prompts

Low

I would be Vice President in California. The year would be May 4, 2024. The President would originally be from Indiana and I would be from California. The head bodyguard would also be from Indiana. Everybody including the president are old middle school friends.

As Vice-President I would be making sure the President made it to places he has to go to on time. I would make sure everybody is doing their job right. I would help the President make the right choices. I would do as much as I can to help the President when he needs help. if the president makes the wrong choice I'll try to make him make the right choice.

The President's name would be Tony DeVille. Me the Vice-President my name if Jimmy Sanderson and the top body guard would be Josh Hollingsworth. The military adviser would be Joe Hanks.

Analysis: Score 2

*This paper focuses on the **topic** but has no conclusion so there is no point for logical order. Vocabulary is basic as are sentence patterns, which have some structural problems. Basic **details** are given with a few examples of what the Vice President would do. The audience connection is not made because the paper is incomplete.*

Today I woke up at 5:00 a.m. and got started on my work. First I had to do all of my paper work. When I got my work done I went to my elevator. I pressed the third floor which is the kitchen. When I got to the kitchen, I made my maid make me a bowl of cereal. I turned on my flat screen and watched ESPN.

Every morning I watch ESPN. I always have to be updated on my sports news. Right when I was about to see Barry Bonds hit his 1,000 home run at age 80 a special announcement came on. The United States is under attack!

Analysis: Score 1

This paper does not focus on the topic of being Vice President, and goes off on other tangents at the end. Logical **order** is there, barely. Vocabulary and sentence structure are basic. General details make up the story, but they are not exceptional supporting details that support the prompt. The tone does not fit the prompt.

Other prompts to be used throughout the school year are found on the following pages.

Name ____________________ **Writing Sample**
Teacher ____________________ **Middle School GR** ___
Date ____________________ **SCORE:**

After School Job

Read the writing prompt below and complete the writing activity.

Lunches are expensive, you spend too much at the mall, you're constantly asking for new clothes, and you like to hang out at the movies with your friends on the weekends. Everything is so expensive that your parents are constantly complaining that you think they are made of money! You decide you will try to get an after-school job.

What kind of job would you like best?
How much money do you think you will make?
How do you think this will help to solve the money problem?
What other problems might the job create?

Write a letter to your parent(s) that persuades them that an after school job is the best solution to the money problem.

Be sure to:

plan your writing before you begin.
include an introduction, a body, and a strong conclusion.
focus on the following ideas:
the kind of job you will try to get
how much you think you will make
problems that may be created or solved
include descriptive details that make your letter persuasive.

Your writing will not be scored on your personal opinions. It will be scored objectively on:

- *how clearly you address the prompt*
- *how well you organize your ideas*
- *how effectively you express yourself*
- *how consistently you use correct paragraphing, grammar, spelling, and punctuation.*

Be sure to use the Standard Rules of English, which do not include slang or jargon.

Name ______________________ **Writing Sample**
Teacher ______________________ **Middle School GR** ___
Date ______________________ **SCORE:**

Cheer Up!

Read the writing prompt below and complete the writing activity.

Mark Twain once said,
"The best way to cheer yourself up is to try to cheer somebody else up."

Write a narrative essay that describes a time when you felt better because you cheered someone else up. Be sure to include why you needed cheering up, what you did to help someone else, and how you felt afterward.

Be sure to:

plan your writing before you begin.
include an introduction, a body, and a strong conclusion.
focus on the following ideas:
why you needed cheering up
what you did to cheer someone else up
how you felt afterward
include descriptive details to make your writing interesting.

Your writing will not be scored on your personal opinions. It will be scored objectively on:

- *how clearly you address the prompt*
- *how well you organize your ideas*
- *how effectively you express yourself*
- *how consistently you use correct paragraphing, grammar, spelling, and punctuation.*

Be sure to use the Standard Rules of English, which do not include slang or jargon.

Name ______________________________ **Writing Sample**
Teacher ______________________________ **Middle School GR** ___
Date ______________________________ **SCORE:**

My Favorite TV Show

Read the writing prompt below and complete the writing activity.

Everyone watches TV, although some people watch more than others. What is your favorite TV show? Is the show enjoyable to all audiences or just people your age? Why is it your favorite?

Write a persuasive essay that convinces someone who has never seen it to watch this show. Be sure to include the name of the show and specific reasons explaining why you like it.

Be sure to:
plan your writing before you begin.
include an introduction, a body, and a strong conclusion.
focus on the following ideas:
the name of the show
specific reasons why you like it
include descriptive details to make your writing interesting.

Your writing will not be scored on your personal opinions. It will be scored objectively on:

- *how clearly you address the prompt*
- *how well you organize your ideas*
- *how effectively you express yourself*
- *how consistently you use correct paragraphing, grammar, spelling, and punctuation.*

Be sure to use the Standard Rules of English, which do not include slang or jargon.

Name ______________________________
Teacher ______________________________
Date ______________________________

Writing Sample
Middle School GR ___
SCORE:

How to Buy a Pair of Jeans

Read the writing prompt below and complete the writing activity.

Your cousin from out of state has just moved in with you. She didn't really bring clothes that you feel are appropriate for your school, so you are going to take her to the mall to buy some jeans. Why does your cousin need jeans? Where is the best place to buy jeans? How should they look and fit?

Write an essay that explains how to buy the perfect pair of jeans. Be sure to include where to get them and how they should look and fit.

Be sure to:

plan your writing before you begin.
include an introduction, a body, and a strong conclusion.
focus on the following ideas:
why your cousin needs jeans
where to go to get them
how they should look and fit
include descriptive details to make your writing interesting

Your writing will not be scored on your personal opinions. It will be scored objectively on:

- *how clearly you address the prompt*
- *how well you organize your ideas*
- *how effectively you express yourself*
- *how consistently you use correct paragraphing, grammar, spelling, and punctuation.*

Be sure to use the Standard Rules of English, which do not include slang or jargon.

Name ______________________
Teacher ______________________
Date ______________________

Writing Sample
Middle School GR ___
SCORE:

The Mysterious Check!

Read the writing prompt below and complete the writing activity.

Yesterday when you got home from school, there was a letter waiting for you. When you opened it, you found a check inside - and nothing else!
What was the value of the check?
Who do you think sent it?
What will you do now?

Write a narrative essay about the day you got the mysterious check in the mail. Be as descriptive as possible.

Be sure to:
plan your writing before you begin.
include an introduction, a body, and a strong conclusion.
focus on the following ideas:
the value of the check
who you think sent it and why
what you will do with the check
include descriptive details to make your writing interesting.

Your writing will not be scored on your personal opinions. It will be scored objectively on:

- *how clearly you address the prompt*
- *how well you organize your ideas*
- *how effectively you express yourself*
- *how consistently you use correct paragraphing, grammar, spelling, and punctuation.*

Be sure to use the Standard Rules of English, which do not include slang or jargon

Name ______________________ **Writing Sample**
Teacher ______________________ **Middle School GR** ___
Date ______________________ **SCORE:**

Just Another Day

Read the writing prompt below and complete the writing activity.

Your life has fallen into a definite routine. Is this a positive or negative thing for you? What do you do on a typical day? What is your life all about? What responsibilities do you have? How do you feel about all of this?

There is a new counselor at school who is trying to get to know all the students. She is also available to anyone who wants to talk to her about peer pressure, stress, school, problems, or just life in general.

Write an essay that describes your daily routine. Make sure you include enough details so that the counselor feels that she knows you a little better.

Be sure to:

plan your writing before you begin.
include an introduction, a body, and a strong conclusion.
focus on the following ideas:
  a detailed description of a typical day in your life
  what your life is really all about
  what responsibilities you have
  how you feel about your life
include exceptional supporting details

Your writing will not be scored on your personal opinions. It will be scored objectively on:

- *how clearly you address the prompt*
- *how well you organize your ideas*
- *how effectively you express yourself*
- *how consistently you use correct paragraphing, grammar, spelling, and punctuation.*

Be sure to use the Standard Rules of English, which do not include slang or jargon

Name ______________________ **Writing Sample**
Teacher ______________________ **Middle School GR** ___
Date ______________________ **SCORE:**

It's Party Time

Read the writing prompt below and complete the writing activity.

Your brother is turning ten in two weeks and has been begging for a birthday party for a few of his close friends. Your mom will be out of town until two days before, and your dad says he is no party planner. That leaves you.

Plan a birthday party for eight 10-year olds that will cost less than $50. What will the guests do? Where will the party be held? What food will be provided? Who will be in charge?

Write an essay that clearly describes your party plan. Be sure to include all the details!

Be sure to:
plan your writing before you begin.
include an introduction, a body, and a strong conclusion.
focus on the following ideas:
a clear description of what the party will be like
who will be in charge
include details to make your essay interesting.

Your writing will not be scored on your personal opinions. It will be scored objectively on:

- *how clearly you address the prompt*
- *how well you organize your ideas*
- *how effectively you express yourself*
- *how consistently you use correct paragraphing, grammar, spelling, and punctuation.*

Be sure to use the Standard Rules of English, which do not include slang or jargon.

Name ______________________
Teacher ______________________
Date ______________________

Writing Sample
Middle School GR ___
SCORE:

Open Mouth, Insert Foot

Read the writing prompt below and complete the writing activity.

From time to time, we all say things we wish we could take back. Can you recall a time you said something that you wish you hadn't? Who was involved? What did you say? How did you try to make up for it?

Write a personal narrative about your experience. Include as many specific details as you can to create a vivid image for your reader. Be sure to include who was involved and what you did to make up for it.

Be sure to:

plan your writing before you begin.
include an introduction, a body, and a strong conclusion.
focus on the following ideas:
What happened
Who was involved
What you did to make up for it
include exceptional supporting details.

Your writing will not be scored on your personal opinions. It will be scored objectively on:

- *how clearly you address the prompt*
- *how well you organize your ideas*
- *how effectively you express yourself*
- *how consistently you use correct paragraphing, grammar, spelling, and punctuation.*

Be sure to use the Standard Rules of English, which do not include slang or jargon.

Name ______________________________ **Writing Sample**
Teacher ______________________________ **Middle School GR** ___
Date ______________________________ **SCORE:**

Equal Opportunities

Read the writing prompt below and complete the writing activity.

John F. Kennedy once said,
"All of us do not have equal talent,
but all of us should have an equal opportunity
to develop our talent."

Think of a time when you were working with someone who was not as talented at something as you are. Do you believe that person should have had the opportunity to participate and further develop his talent?

Write an essay that describes a situation where you were working with someone who was less talented than you. Give reasons why you think people with less talent should or should not be allowed to participate in certain activities.

Be sure to:
plan your writing before you begin.
include an introduction, a body, and a strong conclusion.
focus on the following ideas:
Should all people have equal opportunities to develop their talents?
Why or why not?
include exceptional supporting details.

Your writing will not be scored on your personal opinions. It will be scored objectively on:

- *how clearly you address the prompt*
- *how well you organize your ideas*
- *how effectively you express yourself*
- *how consistently you use correct paragraphing, grammar, spelling, and punctuation.*

Be sure to use the Standard Rules of English, which do not include slang or jargon.

Name	______________________	**Writing Sample**
Teacher	______________________	**Middle School GR ___**
Date	______________________	**SCORE:**

The Lottery

Read the writing prompt below and complete the writing activity.

The evening news has just ended. Your hands are shaking. You heard the numbers, and you've double and triple checked. You have the winning lottery ticket! You have just won a million dollars! How do you feel? What will you do with all the money? How will this change your life and your plans for the future?

Write an essay about the day you won the lottery. Include many specific details, including how you feel, what you will do with the money, and how this might change your life.

Be sure to:

plan your writing before you begin.
include an introduction, a body, and a strong conclusion.
focus on the following ideas:
how you feel
what you will do with the money
how this might change your life
include exceptional supporting details to make your essay interesting.

Your writing will not be scored on your personal opinions. It will be scored objectively on:

- *how clearly you address the prompt*
- *how well you organize your ideas*
- *how effectively you express yourself*
- *how consistently you use correct paragraphing, grammar, spelling, and punctuation.*

Be sure to use the Standard Rules of English, which do not include slang or jargon.

Name ______________________________ **Writing Sample**
Teacher ______________________________ **Middle School GR** ___
Date ______________________________ **SCORE:**

THE TIME CAPSULE

Read the writing prompt below and complete the writing activity.

Your school has been chosen by NASA to select artifacts for a time capsule that would be taken to Mars on the next space mission. Each science student in ninth grade has been asked to identify three artifacts that would be significant to future generations.

Write a letter to the people at NASA describing the three artifacts that you would choose. Describe the artifacts in detail and give specific reasons for why you chose each one.

Be sure to:

plan your writing before you begin.
include an introduction, a body, and a strong conclusion.
focus on the following ideas:
 a detailed description of each artifact
 why you chose them
include exceptional supporting details.

Your writing will not be scored on your personal opinions. It will be scored objectively on:

- *how clearly you address the prompt*
- *how well you organize your ideas*
- *how effectively you express yourself*
- *how consistently you use correct paragraphing, grammar, spelling, and punctuation.*

Be sure to use the Standard Rules of English, which do not include slang or jargon.

Name ______________________________ **Writing Sample**
Teacher ______________________________ **Middle School GR** ___
Date ______________________________ **SCORE:**

Don't Miss This One!

Read the writing prompt below and complete the writing activity.

Reading and movie going are popular teenage activities. Is there a book you have recently read or a movie you have recently seen that you would strongly recommend to your friends? What made this book or movie so memorable?

Write an persuasive essay in which you review the movie or book. Include the title, the names of major characters and a brief summary of the plot. Explain in detail why you thought this movie or book was so special.

Be sure to:
plan your writing before you begin.
include an introduction, a body, and a strong conclusion.
focus on the following ideas:
the name of the movie or book
names and descriptions of the major characters
a brief summary of the book
persuasive reasons why you recommend it to your friends
include exceptional supporting details.

Your writing will not be scored on your personal opinions. It will be scored objectively on:

- *how clearly you address the prompt*
- *how well you organize your ideas*
- *how effectively you express yourself*
- *how consistently you use correct paragraphing, grammar, spelling, and punctuation.*

Be sure to use the Standard Rules of English, which do not include slang or jargon.

Name ______________________ **Writing Sample**
Teacher ______________________ **Middle School GR** ___
Date ______________________ **SCORE:**

Snow Day!!

Read the writing prompt below and complete the writing activity.

It started snowing around midnight. By 7:30 the next morning, there were two feet of snow on the ground and school was canceled. Luckily, the major science project that was due today will now have an extension, because yours is still nowhere near completion.

Suddenly, the phone rings. Your friends are all going skiing! They want to pick you up in about an hour.

Write an essay about what you will do on your snow day. Tell why you made the decision, and explain in detail what you did for the rest of the day.

Be sure to:
plan your writing before you begin.
include an introduction, a body, and a strong conclusion.
focus on the following ideas:
a detailed description of what you decided to do
reasons for your decision
include exceptional supporting details.

Your writing will not be scored on your personal opinions. It will be scored objectively on:

- *how clearly you address the prompt*
- *how well you organize your ideas*
- *how effectively you express yourself*
- *how consistently you use correct paragraphing, grammar, spelling, and punctuation.*

Be sure to use the Standard Rules of English, which do not include slang or jargon.

Name ______________________ **Writing Sample**
Teacher ______________________ **Middle School GR** ___
Date ______________________ **SCORE:**

My Best Friend

Read the writing prompt below and complete the writing activity.

Friends come and go throughout our lives. Coming to a new school, joining a new club, getting a new class schedule, or making a team are all opportunities to make new friends. Do you have a best friend or a close group of friends? How did you meet? What do you do when you are together? What personal qualities do you look for when you choose a best friend?

Write an essay that describes your best friend. Be sure to include how you met, the kinds of things you do together, and the personal qualities you look for in a friend. Include examples and details to make your writing interesting.

Be sure to:

plan your writing before you begin.
include an introduction, a body, and a strong conclusion.
focus on the following ideas:
who your best friend is and how you met
how you spend your time together
the personal qualities you look for in a friend
exceptional supporting details to make your writing interesting.

Your writing will not be scored on your personal opinions. It will be scored objectively on:

- *how clearly you address the prompt*
- *how well you organize your ideas*
- *how effectively you express yourself*
- *how consistently you use correct paragraphing, grammar, spelling, and punctuation.*

Be sure to use the Standard Rules of English, which do not include slang or jargon.

Name	______________________	Writing Sample
Teacher	______________________	Middle School GR ___
Date	______________________	SCORE:

PEER PRESSURE

Read the writing prompt below and complete the writing activity.

Peer pressure is everywhere! One of your friends is always trying to get you to go someplace you shouldn't, to do something you know is wrong, to try something you know is dangerous, or to wear something you know your parents wouldn't approve of or can't afford.

Your teacher has asked you to write an essay about peer pressure. Are you affected by peer pressure? Why or why not? What kind of peer pressure bothers you the most? How do you respond to it?

Be sure to:

plan your writing before you begin.
include an introduction, a body, and a strong conclusion.
focus on the following ideas:
whether or not you are affected by peer pressure
what kind of peer pressure bothers you most
how you respond to peer pressure
include exceptional supporting details.

Your writing will not be scored on your personal opinions. It will be scored objectively on:

- *how clearly you address the prompt*
- *how well you organize your ideas*
- *how effectively you express yourself*
- *how consistently you use correct paragraphing, grammar, spelling, and punctuation.*

Be sure to use the Standard Rules of English, which do not include slang or jargon.

Name ______________________
Teacher ______________________
Date ______________________

Writing Sample
Middle School GR ___
SCORE:

I'm So Stressed Out!

Read the writing prompt below and complete the writing activity.

Teenagers today seem to be faced with more stress than teenagers from past decades. What causes the most stress for you? How do you deal with it? How do you feel when you can't deal with it?

Write an essay that describes how you are affected by stress. Provide supporting details that describe how you deal with stress and how you feel when you can't deal with it.

Be sure to:

plan your writing before you begin.
include an introduction, a body, and a strong conclusion.
focus on the following ideas:
What causes stress?
How do you deal with it?
How do you feel when you can't deal with it?
include exceptional supporting details.

Your writing will not be scored on your personal opinions. It will be scored objectively on:

- *how clearly you address the prompt*
- *how well you organize your ideas*
- *how effectively you express yourself*
- *how consistently you use correct paragraphing, grammar, spelling, and punctuation.*

Be sure to use the Standard Rules of English, which do not include slang or jargon.

Name ______________________________
Teacher ______________________________
Date ______________________________

Writing Sample
Middle School GR ___
SCORE:

Read the writing prompt below and complete the writing activity.

Schools have many rules - sometimes too many. If you could eliminate one rule, what would it be? Why do you think this rule is unnecessary?

Write a persuasive letter to your principal asking him to eliminate a rule that you think is unnecessary. State the rule you think should be eliminated and give at least three reasons that support your decision.

Be sure to:

plan your writing before you begin.
include the parts of a letter
include an introduction, a body, and a strong conclusion.
focus on the following ideas:
Which rule would you eliminate?
Why?
include exceptional supporting details.

Your writing will not be scored on your personal opinions. It will be scored objectively on:

- *how clearly you address the prompt*
- *how well you organize your ideas*
- *how effectively you express yourself*
- *how consistently you use correct paragraphing, grammar, spelling, and punctuation.*

Be sure to use the Standard Rules of English, which do not include slang or jargon.

Name ______________________ **Writing Sample**
Teacher ______________________ **Middle School GR** ___
Date ______________________ **SCORE:**

What a Difference!

Read the writing prompt below and complete the writing activity.

Middle school is much different from elementary school. What differences have you noticed? How have they affected you? Do you prefer middle school over elementary school?

Write a descriptive essay that compares middle school and elementary school. Be sure to include specific differences you have noticed, how they have affected you, and which school setting you prefer.

Be sure to:

plan your writing before you begin.
include an introduction, a body, and a strong conclusion.
focus on the following ideas:
What differences have you noticed?
How have they affected you?
What is your preference?
include exceptional supporting details.

Your writing will not be scored on your personal opinions. It will be scored objectively on:

- *how clearly you address the prompt*
- *how well you organize your ideas*
- *how effectively you express yourself*
- *how consistently you use correct paragraphing, grammar, spelling, and punctuation.*

Be sure to use the Standard Rules of English, which do not include slang or jargon.

Name ______________________
Teacher ______________________
Date ______________________

Writing Sample
Middle School GR ___
SCORE:

Come Join Us!

Read the writing prompt below and complete the writing activity.

Teenagers gather at various places with their friends, and it's sometimes difficult for new students to break into groups that are already established. You decide to write a note to a new student, asking him to meet you and your friends after school. Where do you meet? How will you convince this student to come when he doesn't really know you?

Write a persuasive note that convinces a new student to meet you and your friends at your favorite place. Be sure to say where and be as convincing as you can to make him feel welcome.

Be sure to:
plan your writing before you begin.
include an introduction, a body, and a strong conclusion.
focus on the following ideas:
where you will meet
why he should come
include exceptional supporting details

Your writing will not be scored on your personal opinions. It will be scored objectively on:

- *how clearly you address the prompt*
- *how well you organize your ideas*
- *how effectively you express yourself*
- *how consistently you use correct paragraphing, grammar, spelling, and punctuation.*

Be sure to use the Standard Rules of English, which do not include slang or jargon.

Prompts with Questions for Formal Assessment: High School

Sample Prompt: Making Mistakes

Student Anchor Papers: Student writing samples are included that show examples of papers receiving scores from 1-6. Analysis is included that explains why points were given.

Additional Prompts with Questions for Classroom Use

Title	Genre
Simple Words	Descriptive
The Part-time Job	Persuasive
Hidden Talents	Descriptive
Always Late!	Persuasive
Letter to the Editor	Persuasive
The Courage to Continue	Narrative
My Favorite Restaurant	Persuasive
I Hate to Admit it, but. . .	Descriptive
Life Worth Living	Descriptive
The Bank Account	Expository
Sports	Persuasive
The Worst Time of My Life!	Descriptive
Don't Give Up!	Descriptive
The Best Deal	Persuasive
When I'm 25. . .	Narrative
A Different Kind of Education	Descriptive
My Inspiration	Descriptive
A Tough Choice	Persuasive
Key to the World	Descriptive

Name ______________________________
Teacher ______________________________
Date ______________________________

Writing Sample
High School GR ___
SCORE:

Making Mistakes

Read the writing prompt below and complete the writing activity.

Mary Pickford, a film actress from the early 1900's, once said,

> *"If you have made mistakes . . . there is always another chance for you . . . you may have a fresh start any moment you choose, for this thing we call "failure" is not the falling down, but the staying down."*

Do you agree or disagree with this quotation?

Write an essay that explains your beliefs about the quotation. Support your viewpoint with examples and reasons based on your own experiences, observations, and/or readings.

Be sure to:

plan your writing before you begin.
include an introduction, a body, and a strong conclusion.
focus on the following ideas:
 your viewpoint regarding the quotation
 reasons
include exceptional supporting details.

Your writing will not be scored on your personal opinions. It will be scored objectively on:

- *how clearly you address the prompt*
- *how well you organize your ideas*
- *how effectively you express yourself*
- *how consistently you use correct paragraphing, grammar, spelling, and punctuation.*

Be sure to use the Standard Rules of English, which do not include slang or jargon.

Writing Task: **Making Mistakes**

Student Samples: High School

Huge mistakes can cause serious consequences. Sometimes the damage is irreparable and failure is absolute. Therefore, I am unable to agree with this quote. I will explain in a personal and figurative sense.

Long ago this quote would have especially been proven ineffective. A man who spit at the king's feet had his head cut off, because defiance and weakness were rewarded with death. In the primal world a single mistake could easily have been the last one you made. There are some failures that just cannot be undone.

Falling down is the decline into failure and the act of "giving up". I do not agree with the fact that there is always a way to get back up, or in other words, have a second chance. You cannot expect to have another chance waiting for you after your next failure. A student who goes about their life in high school without any dedication will almost certainly fall into bad habits, finding nothing left for them but the disparaging work in a factory. After giving up those years in high school, there is no way to get them back.

My neighbor has acquired so many DUI's that he will never drive, legally anyway. His chances are already used up. This being something he can never get back, he will have trouble getting and securing a job. No matter what he does, not being able to drive is going to impact his life.

Hopefully you can now see how certain failures can be permanent. This quote is partially flawed in the sense that it is just not true in all cases. For that reason I am totally inclined to disagree with it.

Analysis: Score 5

This paper focuses on the ***topic*** *and has logical* ***order****, even though the conclusion could be stronger.* ***Vocabulary*** *words were strong with* irreparable, figurative, disparaging, and partially flawed. ***Sentence patterns*** *were mostly fluent, but supporting details could have been more developed in paragraphs. Tone and* ***voice*** *are appropriate.*

Writing Task: **Making Mistakes**

Last night, I made a mistake. I decided to go to sleep at three in the morning. Heck, I make a lot of mistakes. For years upon years all I did in school was slack off. Now, I'm a different person. I fully agree with the quote by Mary Pickford that states ". . .there is always another chance for you. . ." To explain to you why I firmly believe this to be true, I'll delve into how everyone has made mistakes, how anyone can learm from them, and finally, how everyone can start over.

See, everyone in the history of the world has made at least one mistake in his lifetime. You don't judge a man if he errors, instead of judge him instead on if he learns or not.

Those who learn from their mistakes are mildly few in number, but with a couple billion people on Earth, they aren't too hard to find. Take a dropout by the name of Dell. He never completed high school. He realized he made a mistake and worked hard to fix it. Now look where he's at. He founded Dell Computers! You could take a college football quarterback and easily see evidence of making mistakes and then learning from them. He missed that pass during the last game, but he nailed it tonight! Even a boy who's missed the bus once might think about it each morning and go out five minutes early from then on.

History shows countless examples of those who didn't learn from their mistakes. Think of Napoleon or Alexander. Rulers who had it great made one too many mistakes, never learned, and paid for it. There's my dog, who still continues to go on the floor. . .or you could look at me; I still forget the bus comes early!

Once shamed, twice shy. . .it's a saying my grandfather says quite often while telling us a World War II story. He worked in loading the Howitzers, and one day, out of carelessness, he dropped a shell. . .on his foot. He's learned to hold on to things a bit better now.

Everyone has the ability to start over. No one is keeping you from trying, only yourself. If you've learned from your mistakes, you know what to do! Even prison mates can change. For proof, watch Dog the Bounty Hunter.

Anyway, the point here is that people make mistakes. To use a common cliché, it makes us human. We can't let ourselves give up, though. If we do, it's only then that we truly fail.

Analysis: Score 3

*This paper focuses on the **topic** of people making mistakes. The logical order point is not given because the sequence of ideas and organization within paragraphs needs improvement. Vocabulary is effective but not outstanding. **Sentence patterns** contribute to fluency, with a few minor exceptions. A connection is made with the **audience**.*

Writing Task: **Making Mistakes**

I agree with this quote because its true. Many people make mistakes and there is always a time where you can have another mistake. There is nothing wrong with making mistakes, its life. Don't put yourself down if you do make mistakes. When you need to worry is when the mistakes happen every day, every time you do something. Don't think of yourself as a bad person just think of it as a learning experience, you learn from your mistakes and move on if they constitley keep happening then its time to do some adjusting in your life change the way you do things. Like the people you hang with and what you do with that crowd of people, it may not always be the easiest thing but its most likely be the best thing you can do. In the long run your mistakes will slowly slip away from your mind and make you a better person. Another thing it might be that your making all these bad mistakes is something may be going on at home and its making you do dumb things. So if you want to make things right the look what people to hang around and change for the better. That's what I think about this quote I hope you enjoyed.

Analysis: Score 2

*This paper generally focuses on the **topic** and **attempts** to provide **details**. Order is lacking, vocabulary is basic, and sentence patterns have structural problems. An attempt is also made to connect with the audience, so I will give a half point for details and a half point for audience for a total of two.*

Writing Task: **Making Mistakes**

Everyone makes mistakes. It's what you do after your mistakes that make you who you are.

I believe that you have one chance to redeem yourself after making any mistake. I strongly believe in second chances. Everyone deserves them. People can do the worst of things but people change, just like life and everything around you. Take now as an example. I dated this guy last year for six months and when we broke up I didn't know why I ever dated him. Hearing all the awful stuff about him that he had done in his life makes me wonder. Just recently we started talking again and I can definitely see that he is someone different from what he used to be.

I know mistakes aren't a good thing but they help you see that there is a little good in everyone if they redeem themself.

Analysis: Score 2

*This paper generally sticks to the **topic** and **attempts** to provide you with **details**.*

Writing Task: **Making Mistakes**

If everybody could go back in time to change any mistake they made, I think everybody would change a mistake they did. What I'll change is the fact that I didn't try in my freshman and sophomore year.

To me the quotation means that no matter what has happened in the past, that's the past. No matter what you have done you can do something different. You can start a new page in your life. Everybody regrets something that they have done in the past. Everybody knows how failure feels like.

I think to everybody failure is like a challenge. It wants to challenge you. You either make it or you fail. I have problems all the time and all with the simple choice of do I succeed or fail. So if anything happens and you fail to that situation don't feel bad. It's just the you lost the challenge.

Analysis: Score 2

This paper generally sticks to the topic and attempts to provide you with details.

The prompts on the following pages are provided for you to use throughout the year.

Name ____________________ **Writing Sample**
Teacher ____________________ **High School GR** ___
Date ____________________ **SCORE:**

Simple Words

Read the writing prompt below and complete the writing activity.

Sometimes single words can express universal ideas. Think about words like loyalty, justice, honor, responsibility, truth, and hope." Which of these words holds the most meaning for you? Why?

Write a descriptive essay explaining which of those words is most meaningful to you. Be sure to include many examples and descriptive details to support your choice.

Be sure to:
plan your writing before you begin.
include an introduction, a body, and a strong conclusion.
focus on the following ideas:
the word that holds the most meaning for you
why the word is meaningful
include exceptional supporting details.

Your writing will not be scored on your personal opinions. It will be scored objectively on:

- *how clearly you address the prompt*
- *how well you organize your ideas*
- *how effectively you express yourself*
- *how consistently you use correct paragraphing, grammar, spelling, and punctuation.*

Be sure to use the Standard Rules of English, which do not include slang or jargon.

Name	____________________	**Writing Sample**
Teacher	____________________	**High School GR ___**
Date	____________________	**SCORE:**

The Part-time Job

Read the writing prompt below and complete the writing activity.

Your homeroom teacher has just announced that she has a list of part-time jobs that will be available during the holidays. She has asked that you choose one and write a persuasive essay on why you would be the best candidate for this job.

What is the job? Why are you the best candidate for this position? What qualities do you possess that will make you a valuable employee?

Write a descriptive essay that explains why you are the best candidate for this job. Include specific details that will make you the top choice.

Be sure to:

plan your writing before you begin.
include an introduction, a body, and a strong conclusion.
focus on the following ideas:
a clear description of the job
persuasive reasons why you would be the best candidate
a description of the qualities you possess
include exceptional supporting details

Your writing will not be scored on your personal opinions. It will be scored objectively on:

- *how clearly you address the prompt*
- *how well you organize your ideas*
- *how effectively you express yourself*
- *how consistently you use correct paragraphing, grammar, spelling, and punctuation.*

Be sure to use the Standard Rules of English, which do not include slang or jargon.

Name ______________________________ **Writing Sample**
Teacher ______________________________ **High School GR** ___
Date ______________________________ **SCORE:**

Hidden Talents

Read the writing prompt below and complete the writing activity.

Benjamin Franklin once said,

"Hide not your talent, they for use were made.
What's a sun-dial in the shade?"

Do you have talent? More specifically, do you have talent in an area that you have not uncovered or worked on to perfect? What's keeping you from it? Why do you think this talent is worth tapping into?

Write a descriptive essay about a talent you have that is not being used. Be sure to include many reasons for why you don't use your talent and descriptive details to describe why this talent might be special.

Be sure to:
plan your writing before you begin.
include an introduction, a body, and a strong conclusion.
focus on the following ideas:
a hidden talent of yours
what is keeping you from realizing it
why this talent might be important
include exceptional supporting details.

Your writing will not be scored on your personal opinions. It will be scored objectively on:

- *how clearly you address the prompt*
- *how well you organize your ideas*
- *how effectively you express yourself*
- *how consistently you use correct paragraphing, grammar, spelling, and punctuation.*

Be sure to use the Standard Rules of English, which do not include slang or jargon.

Name ______________________ **Writing Sample**
Teacher ______________________ **High School GR** ___
Date ______________________ **SCORE:**

Always Late!

Read the writing prompt below and complete the writing activity.

Five students in your homeroom are late for school every morning. They are then assigned after school detention, which makes them late for work at the end of the day. These students just don't seem to be able to get their acts together. One of these students happens to be a very close friend. What causes people to be chronically late? What changes do they need to make in their lives so they will be on time?

Write a note to one of your friends, encouraging him/her to get to school on time. Include organizational tips and suggestions. Give specific details so they know exactly what to do.

Be sure to:

- plan your writing before you begin.
- include an introduction, a body, and a strong conclusion.
- focus on the following ideas:
  - reasons that some people are always late
  - encouraging statements
  - a specific organizational plan
- include exceptional supporting details

Your writing will not be scored on your personal opinions. It will be scored objectively on:

- *how clearly you address the prompt*
- *how well you organize your ideas*
- *how effectively you express yourself*
- *how consistently you use correct paragraphing, grammar, spelling, and punctuation.*

Be sure to use the Standard Rules of English, which do not include slang or jargon.

Name ______________________________ **Writing Sample**
Teacher ______________________________ **High School GR** ___
Date ______________________________ **SCORE:**

Letter to the Editor...

Read the writing prompt below and complete the writing activity.

Because of the large number of teenagers getting into trouble after dark, the mayor has decided to impose a curfew. All students 16 and under will have to be home by 10:00 p.m. starting the beginning of next month.

Write a letter to the editor of your local newspaper stating your feelings about this new rule. Do you agree or disagree with it? What impact will this new rule have on solving the problem? Should any exceptions be made? Give specific examples or why you agree or disagree with the mayor.

Be sure to:

plan your writing before you begin.
include an introduction, a body, and a strong conclusion.
focus on the following ideas:
your opinion about the new rule
an explanation of how it may or may not solve the problem
reasons for having exceptions to the rule
specific reasons for agreeing or disagreeing with the mayor
include exceptional supporting details

Your writing will not be scored on your personal opinions. It will be scored objectively on:

- *how clearly you address the prompt*
- *how well you organize your ideas*
- *how effectively you express yourself*
- *how consistently you use correct paragraphing, grammar, spelling, and punctuation.*

Be sure to use the Standard Rules of English, which do not include slang or jargon.

Name ______________________ **Writing Sample**
Teacher ______________________ **High School GR** ___
Date ______________________ **SCORE:**

Don't Judge a Book by its Cover

Read the writing prompt below and complete the writing activity.

We've all heard the expression, "Don't judge a book by its cover." It is sometimes easier said than done. Have you ever misjudged someone based on his or her appearance?

Write a descriptive essay about what happened, who was involved, and how your feelings about this person changed.

Be sure to:
plan your writing before you begin.
include an introduction, a body, and a strong conclusion.
focus on the following ideas:
what happened
who was involved
how your feelings changed
include exceptional supporting details.

Your writing will not be scored on your personal opinions. It will be scored objectively on:

- *how clearly you address the prompt*
- *how well you organize your ideas*
- *how effectively you express yourself*
- *how consistently you use correct paragraphing, grammar, spelling, and punctuation.*

Be sure to use the Standard Rules of English, which do not include slang or jargon.

Name ______________________________ **Writing Sample**
Teacher ______________________________ **High School GR** ___
Date ______________________________ **SCORE:**

My Favorite Restaurant

Read the writing prompt below and complete the writing activity.

Your high school newspaper is starting a new column that recommends restaurants for teenagers. What is your favorite restaurant? What is the food like? Why do you prefer this restaurant over all the others?

Write a persuasive article about why this restaurant stands out above all the rest.

Be sure to:
plan your writing before you begin.
include an introduction, a body, and a strong conclusion.
focus on the following ideas:
the name of the restaurant
a detailed description of the food
specific reasons why you prefer this restaurant
include exceptional supporting details

Your writing will not be scored on your personal opinions. It will be scored objectively on:

- *how clearly you address the prompt*
- *how well you organize your ideas*
- *how effectively you express yourself*
- *how consistently you use correct paragraphing, grammar, spelling, and punctuation.*

Be sure to use the Standard Rules of English, which do not include slang or jargon.

Name ______________________ **Writing Sample**
Teacher ______________________ **High School GR** ___
Date ______________________ **SCORE:**

I Hate to Admit it, but. . .

Read the writing prompt below and complete the writing activity.

Everyone has something they hate to admit. It might be something they like that no one else does, something they're afraid of, or something they just never wanted to tell anyone.

Write an essay about something you've never wanted to admit. It can be real or imaginary. Just be specific and descriptive.

Be sure to:

plan your writing before you begin.
include an introduction, a body, and a strong conclusion.
focus on the following ideas:
a clear statement of what you hate to admit
reasons why you have never wanted to admit it
include exceptional supporting details

Your writing will not be scored on your personal opinions. It will be scored objectively on:

- *how clearly you address the prompt*
- *how well you organize your ideas*
- *how effectively you express yourself*
- *how consistently you use correct paragraphing, grammar, spelling, and punctuation.*

Be sure to use the Standard Rules of English, which do not include slang or jargon.

Name ______________________ **Writing Sample**
Teacher ______________________ **High School GR** ___
Date ______________________ **SCORE:**

Life Worth Living

Read the writing prompt below and complete the writing activity.

Oliver Wendell Holms, Jr. once said,
"It's faith in something
and enthusiasm for something
that makes life worth living."

What are you enthusiastic about? What makes your life worth living?

Write a descriptive essay that tells what you are most enthusiastic about and why it makes your life worth living. Be sure to include many examples and descriptive details to make writing interesting.

Be sure to:
plan your writing before you begin.
include an introduction, a body, and a strong conclusion.
focus on the following ideas:
what you are enthusiastic about
why it makes your life worth living
include exceptional supporting details.

Your writing will not be scored on your personal opinions. It will be scored objectively on:

- *how clearly you address the prompt*
- *how well you organize your ideas*
- *how effectively you express yourself*
- *how consistently you use correct paragraphing, grammar, spelling, and punctuation.*

Be sure to use the Standard Rules of English, which do not include slang or jargon.

Name ______________________ **Writing Sample**
Teacher ______________________ **High School GR** ___
Date ______________________ **SCORE:**

The Bank Account

Read the writing prompt below and complete the writing activity.

Your parents have just opened a bank account for you. They have put $500 in it and have promised to match any amount you put into it from now until you graduate. What will your goal be? How often will you make deposits? Where will the money come from? What will you do with all the money in the account when you graduate?

Your parents have asked you to write an essay explaining your goal and your plans for the money. They will put this plan in a safety deposit box and give it to you the day you graduate.

Be sure to:

plan your writing before you begin.
include an introduction, a body, and a strong conclusion.
focus on the following ideas:
a goal
a savings plan
an explanation of how you will get the money
what you plan to do with the money when you graduate
include exceptional supporting details

Your writing will not be scored on your personal opinions. It will be scored objectively on:

- *how clearly you address the prompt*
- *how well you organize your ideas*
- *how effectively you express yourself*
- *how consistently you use correct paragraphing, grammar, spelling, and punctuation.*

Be sure to use the Standard Rules of English, which do not include slang or jargon.

Name ______________________ **Writing Sample**
Teacher ______________________ **High School GR** ___
Date ______________________ **SCORE:**

SPORTS

Read the writing prompt below and complete the writing activity.

There are sports during the week, sports on the weekend, sports on TV, sports on radio, sports on video games, sports for girls, sports for boys - basically, sports everywhere!! What's your opinion about sports? Are you an athlete, a spectator, or an uninterested bystander? Why? What are the advantages and disadvantages of being involved (or overcome) by sports?

Write a persuasive essay in which you convince your parents that you should or shouldn't be involved in sports.

Be sure to:

plan your writing before you begin.
include an introduction, a body, and a strong conclusion.
focus on the following ideas:
your opinion about sports in general
your "role" in the world of sports
advantages and/or disadvantages to being involved in sports
persuasive reasons that will convince your parents
include exceptional supporting details

Your writing will not be scored on your personal opinions. It will be scored objectively on:

- *how clearly you address the prompt*
- *how well you organize your ideas*
- *how effectively you express yourself*
- *how consistently you use correct paragraphing, grammar, spelling, and punctuation.*

Be sure to use the Standard Rules of English, which do not include slang or jargon.

Name ______________________ **Writing Sample**
Teacher ______________________ **High School GR** ___
Date ______________________ **SCORE:**

The Worst Time of my Life

Read the writing prompt below and complete the writing activity.

Have you ever had a bad day, a bad job, a bad date, a bad haircut, or just a bad attitude? What happened that made this the worst time of your life? Did the situation improve? How?

Write an essay about the worst time of your life.

Be sure to:
plan your writing before you begin.
include an introduction, a body, and a strong conclusion.
focus on the following ideas:
a description of what happened to make this the worst time of your life
an explanation of how the situation improved
include exceptional supporting details

Your writing will not be scored on your personal opinions. It will be scored objectively on:

- *how clearly you address the prompt*
- *how well you organize your ideas*
- *how effectively you express yourself*
- *how consistently you use correct paragraphing, grammar, spelling, and punctuation.*

Be sure to use the Standard Rules of English, which do not include slang or jargon.

Name ______________________ **Writing Sample**
Teacher ______________________ **High School GR** ___
Date ______________________ **SCORE:**

Don't Give Up

Read the writing prompt below and complete the writing activity.

Sir Winston Churchill once said,
"Success is the ability to go from one failure to another with no loss of enthusiasm."

Think of a famous person who accomplished great things by not giving up. Who would this person be? What did they accomplish by not giving up? What can you learn from this person's experiences?

Write a descriptive essay that tells how a famous person accomplished great things by not giving up. Be sure to describe their accomplishment and what you can learn from their experience.

Be sure to:

plan your writing before you begin.
include an introduction, a body, and a strong conclusion.
focus on the following ideas:
a famous person
their accomplishment
what you can learn from this experience
include exceptional supporting details.

Your writing will not be scored on your personal opinions. It will be scored objectively on:

- *how clearly you address the prompt*
- *how well you organize your ideas*
- *how effectively you express yourself*
- *how consistently you use correct paragraphing, grammar, spelling, and punctuation.*

Be sure to use the Standard Rules of English, which do not include slang or jargon.

Name ______________________ **Writing Sample**
Teacher ______________________ **High School GR** ___
Date ______________________ **SCORE:**

The Best Deal

Read the writing prompt below and complete the writing activity.

Over the holidays your parents said they would give you $3500 toward the purchase or lease of a vehicle. The stipulation is that you have to present them with a detailed plan describing how their money will best be spent before they will give it to you.

Will you buy a used car for less money, lease a car (which would require a down payment and monthly payments), or use the money as a down payment on a new car? New car loans through a bank are usually financed for 12 – 60 months at about 8% interest. Your parents would have to co-sign for the loan. Which deal is the best one for you?

Write an essay to your parents that describes the best choice for you. Be sure to give specific reasons to support your ideas.

Be sure to:

plan your writing before you begin.
include an introduction, a body, and a strong conclusion.
focus on the following ideas:
a detailed plan of how you will use the money
persuasive reasons for why you think this is the best choice
include exceptional supporting details

Your writing will not be scored on your personal opinions. It will be scored objectively on:

- *how clearly you address the prompt*
- *how well you organize your ideas*
- *how effectively you express yourself*
- *how consistently you use correct paragraphing, grammar, spelling, and punctuation.*

Be sure to use the Standard Rules of English, which do not include slang or jargon.

Name ______________________________ **Writing Sample**
Teacher ______________________________ **High School GR** ___
Date ______________________________ **SCORE:**

When I'm 25. . .

Read the writing prompt below and complete the writing activity.

The sky is the limit! If you could be anything you wanted to be, live anywhere in the world, and achieve anything you set your mind to, where would you be at age 25?

Write an essay that describes your goals and how you hope to achieve them.

Be sure to:

plan your writing before you begin.
include an introduction, a body, and a strong conclusion.
focus on the following ideas:
  descriptive details about what you will be doing
  where you will be living
  how you will achieve your goals
include exceptional supporting details

Your writing will not be scored on your personal opinions. It will be scored objectively on:

- *how clearly you address the prompt*
- *how well you organize your ideas*
- *how effectively you express yourself*
- *how consistently you use correct paragraphing, grammar, spelling, and punctuation.*

Be sure to use the Standard Rules of English, which do not include slang or jargon.

Name	______________________	**Writing Sample**
Teacher	______________________	**High School GR ___**
Date	______________________	**SCORE:**

A Different Kind of Education

Read the writing prompt below and complete the writing activity.

Much of our education is learned outside of school. What have you learned outside of school? Did someone teach you, or did you learn it on your own? How has this education impacted your life?

Write an essay that describes something important that you have learned outside of school. Be sure to include what you learned, how you learned it, and how it has impacted your life. Be sure to include exceptional supporting details.

Be sure to:

plan your writing before you begin.
include an introduction, a body, and a strong conclusion.
focus on the following ideas:
descriptive details about what you will be doing
where you will be living
how you will achieve your goals
include exceptional supporting details

Your writing will not be scored on your personal opinions. It will be scored objectively on:

- *how clearly you address the prompt*
- *how well you organize your ideas*
- *how effectively you express yourself*
- *how consistently you use correct paragraphing, grammar, spelling, and punctuation.*

Be sure to use the Standard Rules of English, which do not include slang or jargon.

Name ______________________________ **Writing Sample**
Teacher ______________________________ **High School GR** ___
Date ______________________________ **SCORE:**

My Inspiration

Read the writing prompt below and complete the writing activity.

We all know someone who inspires us to do more and to do better than we ever imagined was possible. Which person inspires you the most? How? Why are you a better person because of knowing or knowing about this individual?

Write an essay that describes the person who inspires you most. Be sure to explain how you are inspired and why you are a better person because of this individual. Include specific examples and descriptive details.

Be sure to:
plan your writing before you begin.
include an introduction, a body, and a strong conclusion.
focus on the following ideas:
the person who inspires you
how they inspire you
why you are a better person because of it
include exceptional supporting details.

Your writing will not be scored on your personal opinions. It will be scored objectively on:

- *how clearly you address the prompt*
- *how well you organize your ideas*
- *how effectively you express yourself*
- *how consistently you use correct paragraphing, grammar, spelling, and punctuation.*

Be sure to use the Standard Rules of English, which do not include slang or jargon.

Name ______________________ **Writing Sample**
Teacher ______________________ **High School GR** ___
Date ______________________ **SCORE:**

A Tough Choice

Read the writing prompt below and complete the writing activity.

TV's, mp3 players, cell phones, and computers entertain students when they are not in school. Your parents have decided to crack down and only allow you to keep one. Which one will you choose? What reasons will you give for choosing that one?

Write an essay about the one you would keep if you had to make a choice.

Be sure to:

plan your writing before you begin.
include an introduction, a body, and a strong conclusion.
focus on the following ideas:
Which one will you choose?
Why?
include exceptional supporting details

Your writing will not be scored on your personal opinions. It will be scored objectively on:

- *how clearly you address the prompt*
- *how well you organize your ideas*
- *how effectively you express yourself*
- *how consistently you use correct paragraphing, grammar, spelling, and punctuation.*

Be sure to use the Standard Rules of English, which do not include slang or jargon.

Name ____________________________
Teacher ____________________________
Date ____________________________

Writing Sample
High School GR ___
SCORE:

The Key to the World

Read the writing prompt below and complete the writing activity.

Jane Hamilton once said,
"It is books that are the key to the wide world;
If you can't do anything else, read all that you can."

How has reading impacted your life? What kinds of things have you learned by reading? How will reading continue to shape your life in the future?

Write an essay that describes how reading has impacted your life. Be sure to include the kinds of things you have already learned as well as how reading will continue to shape your future.

Be sure to:
plan your writing before you begin.
include an introduction, a body, and a strong conclusion.
focus on the following ideas:
how reading has impacted your life
things you have learned by reading about them
how reading will continue to impact your life
include exceptional supporting details.

Your writing will not be scored on your personal opinions. It will be scored objectively on:

- *how clearly you address the prompt*
- *how well you organize your ideas*
- *how effectively you express yourself*
- *how consistently you use correct paragraphing, grammar, spelling, and punctuation.*

Be sure to use the Standard Rules of English, which do not include slang or jargon.

Prompts without Questions for Middle School

Use these prompts as they are, or add questions to match your state format.

My Most Valued Possession

Everyone has a most valued possession, even though it might not be worth a lot of money. Write a descriptive essay about your most valuable possession.

Come Visit!

Your hometown is special for many reasons. Write a persuasive essay that would convince someone to visit your town.

An Incredible Adult

One of the responsibilities that adults have is to be positive role models for children and adolescents. Write an essay that describes the adult who has impacted your life in a positive way.

It's Beautiful to Me

"Beauty is in the eyes of the beholder." Describe something or someone you think is beautiful.

Time for Lunch!

A new policy has been put in place in your middle school, assigning girls and boys to separate lunch hours. Write a persuasive essay that tells whether you agree with this decision or not.

Personal Achievement

Achieving a personal goal is a rewarding experience, and sometimes no one knows about it but you. Write about a time you achieved a personal goal.

The Universal Language

Music is the universal language. Write an essay that tells what that means to you.

The Parent I Hope to Be

Parents have a number of responsibilities – as providers, as role models, and as caretakers. Describe the type of parent you hope to be.

Change!

Change is necessary. However, it is not often easy or well-received. Write a personal narrative that describes something you would like to change.

Sign Up Now!

Your school is thinking of offering mini-courses, which would be held the last hour of the day. Write a persuasive letter that describes the course you would most like to have offered.

The Perfect Sunday Afternoon

Think about what you might do on a perfect Saturday afternoon without spending any money. Describe what you would do.

Scheduling Dilemma

Due to overcrowded schools, your district is thinking of offering two choices for attendance. Choice 1 is the "half day" session, which goes from 6:00 a.m. to noon or noon to 6:00 p.m. Choice 2 is the year round schedule, where you would go to school for nine weeks, and then have four weeks off. Write a persuasive essay that describes your preference.

Love

There are many types of love. Write an essay about a person, place, or thing that you love.

It Wasn't So Bad After All

Write about a time you had to do something you didn't think you would like. In the end, you actually had a good time.

Prompts without Questions: High School

Use these prompts as they are, or add questions to match your state format.

Driving Age Changes!

Next week a bill will be presented in the State Senate that will change the driving age from 16 to18. Write a letter to your State Senator explaining your opinion of this bill.

My Earliest Memory

Think back to your earliest memory as a child. Write a descriptive essay that vividly paints a picture of this memory.

Eliminate This One, Please!

State education budgets have been cut and your school will have to eliminate some of its programs. Write an essay that describes the program on the top of your elimination list.

This is the Place!

Imagine that you could travel anywhere in the world. Write an essay about your dream location.

Uniforms for Everyone

Because students refuse to abide by the rules of the dress code in your school, the School Board is considering required uniforms for all students next fall. Write a persuasive letter to the Board taking a stand on this issue.

The Most Serious Problem

As a high school student you are told that the future is in your hands. Write an essay that describes the most serious problem facing high school graduates today.

I Can Make a Difference

Write a personal narrative about a time you disagreed with something; but rather than complain, you did something about it.

Family Event

Families come in all shapes, sizes, and levels of stability. Describe a family event that left an impression on you.

Just Read!

Reading is the key to learning about people, places, and events you will never visit in person. Write an essay that describes the importance of reading.

It Could Happen

Violent acts have occurred on some high school campuses across the United States. Describe your biggest fear at school and make recommendations for how students could be protected.

Stay in School

Many students drop out before they graduate from high school. Write an essay that describes why you think this happens and some ideas that might keep more students enrolled.

Trading Places

Most students could name a movie star, athlete, musician, or other adult they look up to and maybe even envy. Describe what your day would be like if you traded places with this person.

And the Award Goes to. . .

An award will be given at the end of the year to the outstanding citizen in your class. Describe this person in detail and tell why you think he or she is deserving of this award.

Chance of a Lifetime!

Attendance is a problem in your school. The student council has decided to raise money for an incredible prize that will be offered in a drawing to those students with perfect attendance. Describe the prize and the rules for eligibility.

Ten Theme-based Prompts for Middle School Writers

Theme: Accomplishment
Think of something you have accomplished during your life that was difficult. Write an essay about this activity or event.

Theme: Adolescence
With adolescence comes added pressure and responsibility. How are you handling it?

Theme: Anger
Tell about a time you wish you had controlled your anger.

Theme: Change
Write an essay about something you wish you could change about yourself.

Theme: Differences
Everyone is different. How is this a positive thing?

Theme: Fairness
Describe an event in your life when you thought you were being treated unfairly.

Theme: Friendship
Write a real or fictional essay about a time when you did something extraordinary for a friend or acquaintance.

Theme: Life
What is the best advice you could give a friend for how people should live their lives?

Theme: Peer Pressure
Write a real or fictional essay about a time you gave in to peer pressure or stood up to your friends and said NO.

Theme: Technology
Describe how technology has changed your life.

Ten Theme-based Prompts for High School Writers

Theme: Aging
Describe how people change as they get older.

Theme: Commitment
Write an essay describing what commitment means to you.

Theme: Conflict
Conflict comes in many forms. Describe how conflict can be avoided.

Theme: Criticism
Write an essay that describes how criticism can be a positive thing.

Theme: Decisions
Write an essay about a time you made a poor decision and regretted it later.

Theme: Discovery
Many important inventions have changed people's lives. Describe the invention you think has made the biggest impact in your life.

Theme: Experience
They say, "Experience is the best teacher." Explain how this relates to your life.

Theme: Individuality
Discuss how you express your individuality and why it is important to you.

Theme: Memories
Think back to a moment in time you'll never forget. Reflect on why that moment is so memorable.

Theme: Peace
Is it possible to have world peace?

Theme: Love
What is love?

Chapter 4: Writing Across the Curriculum

When writing is identified as a school improvement goal, all teachers are expected to contribute to student growth. Typically, the English Department is responsible for diagnosis, individual remediation, and the teaching of literary techniques that will enhance writing skills. What about the rest of the teachers? They make up the content-area teaching staff, with some content being academic and some being non-academic. What should these staff members be responsible for in terms of teaching students to write? Schools tend to divide the responsibilities one of two ways:

Choice A: All teachers with a homeroom are responsible for assigning, scoring, and analyzing the data collected from a periodic writing prompt that is given on the same day throughout the entire school.

Pros: Everyone has the same responsibility, and the English Department doesn't feel "dumped on."

Cons: All teachers are not proficient in scoring essays and analyzing writing data, so the information may not be valid. Teachers in non-English departments get defensive because the English teachers aren't doing anything to support their standards.

Choice B: English teachers collect data from formal, periodic prompt assessments, while content-area teachers do the same within their subject area. There are several ways to do this. The preferred method is to write about what is being taught, teaching students to use the content vocabulary as they focus on the development of a concise, well-written paragraph – not a formal essay.

Pros: Content-area teachers can easily integrate the writing task into what they are currently teaching. It can be a task that takes less than ten minutes. *On the following pages, many ideas will be provided.*

Cons: In the absence of strong leadership, many departments just ignore the task. Sometimes non-English teachers feign ignorance when it comes to modeling exemplary responses or helping students with revision strategies. No one with a college degree needs an excuse, and if one of your school improvement strategies is to write across the curriculum, every teacher needs to participate.

Suggestions:

Share the decision-making process in terms of school-wide expectations.
Set realistic goals and expectations.
Once strategies have been determined, plan ahead for implementation.
Organize lesson plans in advance to allow for writing tasks.
Get help from colleagues and take advantage of student expertise.

Preparing for Writing within your Subject Area

Writing proficiency is one small part of teacher certification. Yet many teachers, especially those in the content areas, lack confidence when it comes to teaching writing skills to students. It's merely a matter of focusing on what needs to be done, integrating it with the current lessons, and looking at it with a different attitude. Whether your classes meet daily or in a block schedule, an occasional ten minutes can be spared. Shrink the whole idea of "writing instruction" down to the development of the concise, content-based paragraph.

Suggestions for Getting Started

1. Inform students of the task in advance.

2. Explain the expectation and share a low, average, and high response.

3. Review the five-sentence paragraph.
   - Introduction
   - Body
   - Conclusion

4. Emphasize the importance of using content terminology.

5. Create an exemplary response.

6. Score the student samples.

7. Transfer the information to a Class Analysis Chart.

8. Analyze the data.

9. Based on staff decisions or school improvement strategies, either teach a follow-up lesson or forward the Class Analysis Chart to the School Improvement Chair for follow-up in English classes.

10. Model, explain, and discuss the exemplary response with students.

11. Make copies of student writing that may be used as future examples. These may be either outstanding or lacking in quality.

Tracking the Data

How many classes will be writing?

If each teacher has five classes of thirty students, giving the writing assessment includes administering, scoring, and analyzing data for 150 students! Content-area teachers may balk at this added responsibility. While it is important for all teachers to contribute to the improvement of student writing skills, compromises may have to be reached.

Option 1: All content-area teachers will assess every student they have in class every quarter or other designated time.

Option 2: All students will be assessed in each subject area twice a year. Teachers will rotate their own classes, making sure all students are assessed – but not necessarily at the same time.

Option 3: Each teacher will choose one class that will be assessed and tracked throughout the year. Teachers will collaborate at each grade level to make sure no students are missed.

Option 4: Teachers whose classes last only nine weeks (rather than a semester) will collaborate with other nine-week course teachers to determine where and when assessment will take place.

Option 5: ____

____

Option 6: ____

____

How often will assessment occur?

The number of times content-area teachers are responsible for having students write will be determined by the school improvement plan. Starting out, it may be as simple as a baseline sample, a mid-year sample, and a final sample. Strategies that might include modeling, discussing, and teaching specific paragraph design skills would be presented throughout the year at the teacher's discretion.

After the first year, the improvement team (with staff input) will determine the number of writing samples required by each department. Year two might be: baseline, first quarter, midyear, third quarter, and final. These samples may all be of the same type or varied throughout the year. They should be labeled on the Quarterly Tracking Chart for Content-based Writing. Samples should also be kept throughout the school year, organized by quarter or by class.

How soon do the data reports have to be turned in, and to whom?

If, according to the school improvement plan, teachers are required to assess students five times a year (baseline, quarter one, quarter two, quarter three, and final), here is a possible scenario:

Baseline: Assessment is given during the first week of school.
(Keep originals or copies for accreditation documentation.)
Scores are due by Friday of the second week.
Feedback is given by administrator by Friday of the third week.

Quarter 1: Assessment is given during the 7th week.
(Keep originals or copies for accreditation documentation.)
Scores are due by Friday of the 8th week.
Feedback is given by administrator by Friday of the 9th week.

Quarter 2: Repeat Quarter 1 Procedures

Quarter 3: Repeat Quarter 2 Procedures

Final: Final assessment is given during the 5th week.
(Keep originals or copies for accreditation documentation.)
Scores and yearly tracking charts are due by Friday of the 6th week.
Feedback is given by administrator by Friday of the 7th week.

How is content-based writing scored?

Once the content-based writing task is completed, the student samples need to be scored. The only difference between using The Simple 6™ to score formal essays and shorter, content-based writing is length. Instead of looking for three or more examples of "evidence of mastery", there will probably only be one or two. Just use the mini rubric that is provided. Always have them available in your class for student use.

REMEMBER: The same thoughts would go through the scorer's mind no matter how long the piece is.

Does this writing focus on the topic, following the directions for the task?
Is it in order (introduction, three detail sentences, and conclusion)?
Is there evidence of precise, content-based vocabulary?
Are the sentences varied so that the paragraph is fluent and easy to read?
Do the detail sentences support the topic, giving specific examples and descriptions?
Was the paragraph written in a tone that was appropriate for the task?
(This usually means formal and informational rather than informal and conversational.)

Documents Needed for Writing across the Curriculum

These documents will guide you through the writing assessment process. Templates are provided on the following pages.

Writing Task Template

A generic writing task template has been provided that can be used in any subject area. The task description and student writing would go on the same page. If you prefer using index cards or other formats, you may use the template as a transparency so students are totally clear about the expectations.

Mini Rubric

The four rubrics per page are designed to be cut apart and used as a guide for students or an assessment tool for teachers. A mini rubric should be attached to each student writing sample.

Class Analysis Chart

A Class Analysis Chart should be filled out for each class of students being assessed. Last names of students are listed alphabetically and score points from the mini rubric are transferred. Teachers then examine and analyze the data derived from the writing exercise.

Weaknesses found might be addressed within the subject area or passed on to the English Department for further skill instruction. Again, this would be determined by the school improvement plan.

Completed Class Analysis Chart

A completed Class Analysis Chart has been provided to use as a guide.

Quarterly Tracking Chart

The purpose of the Quarterly Tracking Chart is to self-evaluate or document quarterly progress in terms of the percentage of students passing each assessment. This completed document may be required each quarter for grade level or building level tracking.

Yearly Class Record

Teachers may be asked to complete this chart for yearly data collection. It illustrates yearly progress of individual students.

Subject: ______________

Name: ____________________
Date: ____________________
Class: ____________________

WRITING TASK: ____
____

Write a concise paragraph that:

- introduces the topic
- provides specific, content-based details
- uses jargon or precise vocabulary from the subject area
- has a concluding statement

You may choose to write a paragraph that only contains five sentences.
Know, however, that your paragraph will be assessed on the following:

- *Did you focus on the assigned topic?*
- *Are your thoughts in order?*
- *Did you include challenging, content-based vocabulary?*
- *Are sentence patterns varied to avoid a list-like paragraph?*
- *Did you provide exceptional content-based, supporting details?*
- *Is the tone of the writing appropriate for the task?*

Planning Space: Use the back of this page to plan your writing.

The Simple 6™

0 / 1

___ Focus on the Topic
___ Logical Order
___ Challenging Vocabulary
___ Varied Sentence Patterns
___ Exceptional Supporting Details
___ Audience

___ TOTAL POINTS

Kay Davidson, Revised 2002

The Simple 6™

0 / 1

___ Focus on the Topic
___ Logical Order
___ Challenging Vocabulary
___ Varied Sentence Patterns
___ Exceptional Supporting Details
___ Audience

___ TOTAL POINTS

Kay Davidson, Revised 2002

The Simple 6™

0 / 1

___ Focus on the Topic
___ Logical Order
___ Challenging Vocabulary
___ Varied Sentence Patterns
___ Exceptional Supporting Details
___ Audience

___ TOTAL POINTS

Kay Davidson, Revised 2002

The Simple 6™

0 / 1

___ Focus on the Topic
___ Logical Order
___ Challenging Vocabulary
___ Varied Sentence Patterns
___ Exceptional Supporting Details
___ Audience

___ TOTAL POINTS

Kay Davidson, Revised 2002

Secondary Class Analysis Chart

TASK: ______________________________ **DATE** __________

NAMES	TOPIC	ORDER	VOCAB	PATTERNS	DETAILS	AUDIENCE	TOTAL

Comments / Reflection:

Secondary Class Analysis Chart

TASK: SCIENCE TEST ESSAY PHOTOSYNTHESIS **DATE** 10.10.07

NAMES	TOPIC	ORDER	VOCAB	PATTERNS	DETAILS	AUDIENCE	TOTAL
ADAMS	1	1	1	1	1	1	6
BAKER	1			1	1		3
CARTER	1	1		1	1		4
DONNELLY	1	1			1		3
EVANS	1	1			1		3
FISHER	1	1	1	1	1	1	6
HALL	1	1		1			3
JACKSON	1	1		1		1	4
LOWER	1	1	1	1	1	1	6
LUTZ	1	1			1		3
MANNING	1	1	1	1	1	1	6
MENDEZ	1	1	1		1		4
MILLER	1	conc		1	1	1	4
NIXON	1	1			1		3
NOTTINGHAM	1	1	1	1	1	1	6
OBRIEN	1	1	1	1			4
OSBORNE	1	1	1	1	1		5
PORTER	1	1			1		3
RODRIGUEZ	1	1			1		3
SANCHEZ	1	1		1		1	4
SANDERS	1		1	1	1		4
SHELTON	1	conc	1		1		3
STANTON	1	conc	1	1	1	1	5

Comments / Reflection:

Use more vocabulary from unit.
Tone should be more formal.
Model concluding sentence.

English Dept.: Sentence Patterns

QUARTERLY TRACKING CHART FOR CROSS CURRICULAR WRITING

Task ______________ **Class** ______________ **Date** ________ **% Passing** _________

	# of Students	Score 0 N %	Score 1 N %	Score 2 N %	Score 3 N %	Score 4 N %	Score 5 N %	Score 6 N %
(6) Writing Application								
(4) Lang. Conventions								

Task ______________ **Class** ______________ **Date** ________ **% Passing** _________

	# of Students	Score 0 N %	Score 1 N %	Score 2 N %	Score 3 N %	Score 4 N %	Score 5 N %	Score 6 N %
(6) Writing Application								
(4) Lang. Conventions								

Task ______________ **Class** ______________ **Date** ________ **% Passing** _________

	# of Students	Score 0 N %	Score 1 N %	Score 2 N %	Score 3 N %	Score 4 N %	Score 5 N %	Score 6 N %
(6) Writing Application								
(4) Lang. Conventions								

TEACHER ____________________________________ **GR. LEVEL** _____ **YEAR** ________

YEARLY CLASS RECORD: Writing Across the Curriculum

GRADES 6-12

Subject: ________ Year: ________ Teacher: ________

STUDENT NAMES	BASELINE:AUG.	TASK 1: OCT.	TASK 2: JAN.	TASK 3: MAR.	FINAL: MAY
% PASSING					

What if all teachers are expected to work on revision strategies with students?

The single most important activity any content-area teacher can do to improve written responses is to model an exemplary response and explain why it is considered an exemplar. Don't have an exemplary response? Then you will have to write one. Think of it as the model you would use when scoring an essay question on an exam. The first sentence should address the topic. The second, third, and fourth sentences should provide specific details about the subject – sometimes in a specific order. The last sentence should summarize the topic or be reflective in nature.

Content-area teachers usually have two main concerns:

First, what if the information in the paragraph is not correct? The easy answer to this is to score the piece for writing proficiency only. If content is being scored for correctness, that is a separate grade that may or may not be taken within your subject area. If this is a big issue, exchange papers with someone in another department.

What about conventions? Many teachers don't feel qualified to make judgments regarding capitalization, spelling, and punctuation (especially the use of commas). Consider making a general assessment (+ / –) to indicate minimal or many errors. Again, this staff decision should be documented in your school improvement plan.

Tips for Revision in the Content Areas

If teachers in non-English departments stop after the writing assessment has been given, only half the task has been accomplished. Students will only show improvement if the assessment has been read carefully, scored, and analyzed on a Class Analysis Chart. Once weaknesses are identified, further action is necessary.

1. If nothing else, review the task with students and show them the exemplary response that was expected.

2. Share student samples (preferably from a different class) and talk about why the samples were deficient.

3. Provide students with a Score 2 or 3 paper that was written by you or an anonymous student, and give students time to revise and discuss.

4. If specific, content-based details are weak, provide students with more questions in the task to guide the body of their paragraphs.

5. Model the entire procedure with each class, getting ideas from students as you write together.

The Cross-Curricular Writing Task

The Format: What might these writing responses look like?

INDEX CARD

For some teachers, the shorter it appears to be, the better. At least use index cards that are the 4x6 or 5x8 size. Students already write small enough, and there is no point in contributing to the readability problem. Have students put their name (last name first) in the upper left, followed by the date in the upper right. Skip a line and center the title, capitalizing appropriately. Skip another line, indent, and begin writing.

TEST RESPONSE

Obviously, this response will be part of a formal assessment in your particular subject area. It will probably not be a task that is collected and saved separately, as other tasks might be. Instead, it will remain in the test's body, scored first as part of the test for content correctness, and secondly (or later) as a writing response only. Students should be informed in advance that a writing score will be derived from the essay portion of the test.

If there is only going to be one essay question on the test, tell students in advance what it will be. If you can't allow yourself to do that, then tell students it will be one of the following questions and give them three choices. If that doesn't work for you, at least tell students the general topic of the essay so they have half a chance of being able to write intelligently about it.

Remember: the purpose of essay questions is to assess student understanding of main concepts that were taught during the unit of study. If you have been organized and thorough in your teaching, students should be able to tell *you* what the essay's main focus will be.

WRITING TASK TEMPLATE

In each of the following subject areas, writing ideas and response sheets have been provided. They make the task clear to those students who need visual as well as auditory instructions, offer reminders to students, and provide enough lines for students to write a concise, content-based paragraph.

BLANK PAPER

I can't begin to predict the different types of writing tasks that might be assigned across the diverse curriculum in a middle or high school. Some types of writing will take much more time and space than a ten-minute writing task that is done on an index card. It just depends on the subject area, the subject's writability factor, and the teacher's creativity and higher level thinking style.

The following pages give ideas for writing assignments across the curriculum, templates for writing response tasks, and sample student responses.

Applications for Writing in Other Academic Areas

Math
Reflect on today's lesson. What did you learn?
Explain how you answered one homework problem.
Write a problem solving scenario for others to solve.

____

____

____

Science
Explain a scientific process.
Respond to an essay question on exams with a complete paragraph.
Take extensive lab notes that include questions, inferences, and hypotheses.

____

____

____

Social Studies
Write a brief summary of an historical event.
Write a persuasive speech about a school policy.
Write an editorial about a political issue.

____

____

____

Foreign Language/Cultures
Describe a foreign tradition that is not seen in the U.S.
Reflect on how difficult it is to become fluent in another language.
Persuade your parents to let you study for a semester in a foreign country so you can become more fluent in speaking the language.

____

____

____

PE/Health
Describe a healthy way to lose ten pounds.
Explain how to play. . . (any game)
Explain why it is important to exercise.

____

____

____

Business
Explain how finance relates to everyday life.
Describe how technology has affected the business world.
Imagine you have employees. Describe your management style.

____

____

____

Fine Arts
Describe the style of a particular artist or musician.
Write about your favorite musicians or artists.
Reflect on how certain types of music or art make you feel.

____

____

____

Family and Consumer Science
Describe how to make a favorite recipe.
Explain the importance of good nutrition.
Describe what it takes to be a responsible parent.

____

____

____

Industrial Technology
Describe the safety factors to be considered when using power tools.
Summarize what you have learned about building your own house.
Describe how to measure for carpeting.

____

____

____

Writing Across the Curriculum in MATH

Remember:
- Implementation of The Simple 6™ should be done in Language Arts classes.
- The students in your classes know the program. Let them help you.

When writing about MATH:
- Always use The Simple 6™ components. Call them by name.
- Refer to your classroom poster throughout the year.
- Focus on the development of the concise, content-based paragraph.
- Recognize the value in 10-15 minute opportunities to write: essay questions, reflections, critiques, opinions, etc.
- Set a monthly or quarterly goal *(personal or as per school improvement plan.)*
- Score the writing using The Simple 6™ mini rubric.
- Analyze and turn in data.
- Model appropriate responses so students get a better understanding of the exemplary expectation.

IDEAS FOR WRITING ABOUT MATH

Reflect on today's lesson. What did you learn?
Explain how you answered one homework problem. Focus on showing your work. (Designate same problem for all students.)
Write a problem-solving scenario based on the content or topic just covered.

ADDITIONAL WRITING ACTIVITIES FOR MATH:

1.

2.

3.

A general weakness I see in writing about MATH is:

____

____

____

MATH

Name: ____________________
Date: ____________________
Class: ____________________

WRITING TASK: *What did you learn during today's math lesson?*

Write a concise paragraph that:

- introduces the topic
- provides content-based details about what you learned
- uses some of the mathematical terms you heard today
- has a concluding statement, possibly including where you need help or what you felt was most important

You may choose to write a paragraph that only contains five sentences. Know, however, that your paragraph will be assessed on the following:

- *Did you focus on the assigned topic?*
- *Are your thoughts in order?*
- *Did you include precise, mathematical vocabulary?*
- *Did you vary sentence patterns to avoid a list-like paragraph?*
- *Did you provide exceptional, content-based, supporting details?*
- *Is the tone of your writing appropriate for the task?*

Planning Space: Use the back of this page to plan your writing.

Writing about Math

Writing Task: What did you learn during today's math lesson?
Student Samples: Solving Equations

High

Today in algebra we learned how to solve equations with variables on both sides of the equal sign. It's a lot like solving simpler equations, but you need to combine the variable terms first. You can combine them either by bringing the variable from the left side of the equation to the right, or by bringing the variable from the right side to the left. It is important to think it through in advance so that you end up with a positive coefficient of the variable term no matter on which side of the equation it ends up. This skill will add to my ability to solve many different kinds of equations.

Analysis: Score 6

*This paragraph focuses on the **topic**, has **order**, and uses appropriate mathematical **terms**. **Sentences** are complex and create to overall fluency. **Supporting details** have been provided, and the conclusion is sufficient. **Tone** is appropriate for the task.*

Average

We are learning how to solve equations. Today the equations had variables on both sides of the equal sign. You have to get the numbers on one side and the variables on the other side in order for it to work out. Can you help me to figure out where to start? I don't know if I should go to the left or the right.

Analysis: Score 3

*This paragraph focuses on the **topic** and provides basic **details**. The conclusion is missing, so no point is given for logical order.* Variable *and* equation *are words from the lesson, but other opportunities to use more precise vocabulary were not taken. No point was given for lower level sentences. The piece has the appropriate **tone** for someone that is requesting help.*

Low

Today in math I learned about solving equations. It was pretty easy. I was able to fully comprehend that you move the variable. I have a bad headache, sorry.

Analysis: Score 1

*A minimal **attempt** is made to focus on the **topic,** so one attempt point is given. Having a headache causes this student to lose five points.*

Writing about Math

Writing Task: What did you learn during today's math lesson?
Student Samples: Pythagorean Theorem

Today in Geometry class I learned about the Pythagorean Theorem, which was invented by a man named Pythagoras, who lived in ancient Rome. The theorem states that in a right triangle the square of the length of the hypotenuse is equal to the sum of the squares of the lengths of the legs. In an acute triangle, the sum of the legs squared is more than the hypotenuse, but in an obtuse triangle the sum of the legs squared is less than the hypotenuse. I also learned that a triangle is only a triangle if, when the total of the smallest sides is , its total is more than the third side. I now feel confident that I can solve any triangle problem that comes my way.

Analysis: Score 6 *This paragraph focuses on the **topic,** has **logical order** and uses appropriate **mathematical terms**. **Sentences** are complex and create fluency, **details** are precise and content-based, and the **tone** is appropriate.*

Today in math we learned about the Pythagorean Theorem and its converse. The theorem states that the sum of the squares of both legs equals the square of the hypotenuse. We also learned how to use the Pythagorean Theorem to solve areas and to determine whether you are working with a right, acute, or obtuse triangle. Overall, I learned a lot of new information about the Pythagorean Theorem that I didn't know, and I understand it quite well.

Analysis: Score 5 *This paper focuses on the **topic**, has **order**, and uses **mathematical terms**. **Sentence structure** creates fluency, and the **tone** is appropriate. The exceptional supporting details could have been more precise and inclusive, so no point was given. (If teachers feel that these details are inclusive, it would be a Score 6.)*

We studied two new sections in geometry today which covered the Pythagorean Theorem. These sections also included the method for computing the area of a triangle and the three types of triangles. The three kinds were right, acute, and obtuse. I understand some of it, maybe all of it. The parts that confused me were the ones with the area of a triangle and how to solve it inside the Pythagorean Theorem. I did learn a lot today, but another review tomorrow would be helpful.

Analysis: Score 3 *This paragraph focuses on the **topic** to a degree, has **logical order**, and uses the **vocabulary** from the lesson. Sentence patterns have faulty structure, details are weak, and the tone is too informal.*

Today in math we learned about the Pythagorean Theorem and its converse. I learned different ways to plug in numbers to the formula. I also learned that the legs are A and B and the hypotenuse is C. In conclusion I think I will do well on this. I just need to apply it on the test.

Analysis: Score 2 *This paragraph focuses on the **topic** and has **logical order**. Vocabulary is not used to enhance details, sentence patterns are low level, details are not specific enough, and the tone is too informal.*

During math class today I didn't learn anything new. The Pythagorean Theorem was taught to me earlier than high school. Our teachers did a good job of explaining it though.

Analysis: Score 1 *This student makes a meager **attempt** to focus on the **topic**. No other useful information is given.*

Today in math class I tried to learn the Pythagorean Theorem. It did not go very well because I still didn't really know it. Okay, well I am just going to give up on writing about this math stuff, so I am just going to say hi! how are you? I'm good. okay I have to go do my homework now!

Analysis: Score 0 *This student clearly doesn't know enough about the Pythagorean Theorem to even articulate where her weaknesses are. Since she runs away with other (social) ideas, she receives no points.*

Writing Across the Curriculum in SCIENCE

Remember:

- Implementation of The Simple 6™ should be done in Language Arts classes.
- The students in your classes know the program. Let them help you.

When writing about SCIENCE:

- Always use The Simple 6™ components. Call them by name.
- Refer to your classroom poster throughout the year.
- Focus on the development of the concise, content-based paragraph.
- Recognize the value in 10-15 minute opportunities to write: essay questions, reflections, critiques, opinions, etc.
- Set a monthly or quarterly goal *(personal or as per school improvement plan).*
- Score the writing using The Simple 6™ mini rubric.
- Analyze and turn in data.
- Model appropriate responses so students get a better understanding of the exemplary expectation.

IDEAS FOR WRITING ABOUT SCIENCE

Explain a scientific process.
Write complete paragraphs when responding to essay questions on exams.
Prepare in advance.
Take extensive lab notes that include questions, inferences, and hypotheses.

ADDITIONAL WRITING ACTIVITIES FOR SCIENCE:

1.

2.

3.

A general weakness I see in writing about SCIENCE is:

____

____

____

SCIENCE

Name: ____________________
Date: ____________________
Class: ____________________

WRITING TASK: Explain a scientific process or idea of your choice.

Write a concise paragraph that:

- introduces the topic
- provides specific, content-based supporting details
- uses precise scientific jargon or terminology
- has a concluding statement

You may choose to write a paragraph that only contains five sentences.
Know, however, that your paragraph will be assessed on the following:

- *Did you focus on the assigned topic?*
- *Are your thoughts in order?*
- *Did you include precise, scientific vocabulary?*
- *Did you vary sentence patterns to avoid a list-like paragraph?*
- *Did you provide exceptional scientific details?*
- *Is the tone of your writing appropriate for the task?*

Planning Space: Use the back of this page to plan your writing.

Writing about Science

Writing Task: Explain a scientific process or idea of your choice.
Student Samples: Scientific Process

High

Embryonic stem cell research is a topic of ethical debate that many scientists and theologians cannot agree on. One of the main topics discussed is the point in time an embryo becomes a human being. From a theologian's stand point, once sperm and egg meet, a zygote is formed, the earliest form of an embryo. Some scientists, however, disagree with this opinion. Many scientists believe that an embryo is not a human because of the absence of a nervous system and human-like features. This debate becomes very personal. Should we murder embryos to save lives or should we use the resources we already have to learn more about the human body?

Analysis: Score 6

*This paragraph focuses on the **topic**, has logical **order**, and uses scientific **vocabulary**. **Sentences** are fluent, **details** are provided, and the **tone** is appropriate.*

Average

Have you ever needed to find the density of something? It is quite simple actually, all you have to do is divide the objects mass by its volume. To find the mass you place it on a scale and write down the readings. Its volume is found either by placing it in a fluid and doing the calculations or by multiplying its length, width, and height. Density may be very useful to you some day.

Analysis: Score 3

*The paragraph focuses on the **topic**, has **logical order**, and uses **vocabulary** related to the concept of density. Sentence patterns are lower level, details could be more precise, and tone is too familiar.*

Low

One of the most popular experiments that most kids did when they were young is the mouse and maze experiment. First you make four mazes and put a piece of cheese. Each maze has a different level. You then use a stopwatch to count the time it takes the mouse. This is my favorite experiment.

Analysis: Score 2

*This student focuses on the **topic** of a favorite science experiment. The paper has **logical order**, but no vocabulary, no complex sentence patterns, and no scientific details. The tone of the paper is too informal.*

SCIENCE

Name: ____________________
Date: ____________________
Class: ____________________

WRITING TASK: Write a concise paragraph that summarizes what you learned during our last unit of study.

Write a concise paragraph that:

- introduces the topic
- provides specific, content-based supporting details
- uses precise scientific jargon or terminology
- has a concluding statement

You may choose to write a paragraph that only contains five sentences. Know, however, that your paragraph will be assessed on the following:

- *Did you focus on the assigned topic?*
- *Are your thoughts in order?*
- *Did you include precise, scientific vocabulary?*
- *Did you vary sentence patterns to avoid a list-like paragraph?*
- *Did you provide exceptional scientific details?*
- *Is the tone of your writing appropriate for the task?*

Planning Space: Use the back of this page to plan your writing.

Writing Across the Curriculum

Writing Task: Write a concise paragraph that summarizes what you learned during our last unit of study.

Student Samples: Sharks

The shark is a majestic creature, ancient and powerful. Rows of razor-sharp teeth contribute to its reputation for being the deadliest predator in the ocean. Sharks tend to be slow movers, but attack with lightning speed and kill without hesitation. Many sharks are blamed for human losses and are therefore hunted, but none more than the Great White, which actually feeds on seals and penguins. Humans tend to be accidental food, but if you are swimming in the ocean remember this: If you see it, it probably sees you.

Analysis: Score 6

*This paper focuses on the **topic**, has **logical order**, and uses challenging **vocabulary** (although not necessarily content-related). **Sentence patterns** contribute to overall fluency, **details** are informational, and **tone** is appropriate for the task.*

Sharks are in the order Condrichthyes, along with skates and rays. They have cartilaginous exoskeletons and a persistent notochord. They have a very complex brain, with two olfactory lobes, two cerebral hemispheres, two optical lobes, a cerebellum, and a medulla oblongata. The sexes are separate and fertilization is internal. They have a heterocercal caudal fin and a complex circulatory system.

The anatomy of the shark is interesting, unique, and something I plan to study more in depth.

Analysis: Score 6

*The paragraph focuses on the **topic**, has **logical order**, and uses **vocabulary** specific to the subject. **Sentences** are complex and fluent, **details** are scientific, and **tone** is appropriately informational.*

Sharks, for the most part, are not as deadly as people think. Most sharks won't attack people in the water for no good reason, normally. They don't usually attack for consummation purposes. Sharks like the smell of blood, and therefore may attack if someone in the water is bleeding. Normally, the only other time a shark would attack is if it feels threatened. This explains why sharks are not as deadly as people think.

Analysis: Score 2

*The paragraph focuses on the **topic** and has **order**. The lower-level details are "general knowledge" and not indicative of high school level content. Vocabulary is not scientific, sentence patterns do not contribute to overall fluency, and tone is too familiar.*

Have you ever been scared while swimming in the ocean? This is partly due to the incredible animal the shark. The shark is a very misunderstood animal. it is called the killer, and many other names due to attacks on humans. It is sad because hundreds of sharks are killed to one shark attack. The shark attack due to the misinterpreting, like it mistakes a human on a surf board as a seal etc. If humans are one of the sharks prey than why do they bite and then let go? 9/10 of the time a shark bites and lets go because humans are not a part of their diet. This is a few reasons that sharks are misunderstood by humans.

Analysis: Score 2

*This paragraph focuses on the **topic** and has **order**. Vocabulary is not scientific in nature, sentence patterns have serious structural problems, details are low level, and the tone is too familiar.*

Sharks are mysterious creatures. They stick near the shore, and swim great distances. Also they are always moving. There are many things we still have to learn about sharks.

Analysis: Score 2

This paper focuses on the topic and has order. It lacks scientific vocabulary, fluid sentence patterns, and specific details. The tone is too informal.

I don't know too much about sharks but I do know that they can get to a great size. They are a grey color to a blue color. They have rows and rows of teeth their tail fin swings back and forth with their body to make them move faster through the water. They could possible eat you alive if they wanted too. And Jaws is pretty much all about sharks, but it is still a good movie.

Analysis: Score 1

This paper loses the point for focusing on the topic when it concludes with "Jaws." The conclusion also causes it to miss the logical order point. Vocabulary is not science related, sentences are low level, and tone is too informal. One point is given for attempting to provide details, even though they are elementary level.

Writing Across the Curriculum in SOCIAL STUDIES

Remember:

- Implementation of The Simple 6™ should be done in Language Arts classes.
- The students in your classes know the program. Let them help you.

When writing about SOCIAL STUDIES:

- Always use The Simple 6™ components. Call them by name.
- Refer to your classroom poster throughout the year.
- Focus on the development of the concise, content-based paragraph.
- Recognize the value in 10-15 minute opportunities to write: essay questions, reflections, critiques, opinions, etc.
- Set a monthly or quarterly goal *(personal or as per school improvement plan).*
- Score the writing using The Simple 6™ mini rubric.
- Analyze and turn in data.
- Model appropriate responses so students get a better understanding of the exemplary expectation.

IDEAS FOR WRITING ABOUT SOCIAL STUDIES

Write a brief summary of an historical event.

Write a persuasive speech about a school policy.

Write an editorial about a political issue.

ADDITIONAL WRITING ACTIVITIES FOR SOCIAL STUDIES:

1.

2.

3.

A general weakness I see in writing about SOCIAL STUDIES is:

____

____

____

SOCIAL STUDIES

Name: ____________________
Date: ____________________
Class: ____________________

WRITING TASK: *Write a brief summary of an historical event.*

Write a concise paragraph that:

- introduces the topic
- provides specific, content-based supporting details
- uses precise geographical, political, or historical terminology
- has a concluding statement

You may choose to write a paragraph that only contains five sentences.
Know, however, that your paragraph will be assessed on the following:

- *Did you focus on the assigned topic?*
- *Are your thoughts in order?*
- *Did you include challenging vocabulary?*
- *Did you vary sentence patterns to avoid a list-like paragraph?*
- *Did you provide exceptional supporting details?*
- *Is the tone of your writing appropriate for the task?*

Planning Space: Use the back of this page to plan your writing.

Writing in Social Studies

Writing Task: Write a brief summary of an historical event.

Student Samples: The Constitutional Convention

High

The Constitutional Convention was held in Phillidelphia in 1787. Twelve of the thirteen states sent delegates to the convention, with Rhode Island being the exception. The goal was to establish a constitution for the United States that would give the people the power and still provide a strong national government. After much arguing and debate between the small and the larger states, the Great Compromise solved most of the problems. The end of the Convention was marked by the ratification of the Constitution by nine states, and the designation of George Washington as the first President.

Analysis: Score 6

*This paper is totally **focused**, has great **organization**, and uses specific **vocabulary** for the subject: delegates, establish, ratification, designation. **Sentence patterns** provide fluency, specific content-related **details** are provided, and the formal **tone** is appropriate.*

Average

In the summer of 1787 fifty-five men gathered together to discuss a new government that could meet the needs of the nation. These delegates were smart and experienced men. They are now known as the framers of the Constitution. By the end of the convention 30 delegates had signed the Constitution. It took almost an entire year for the Constitution to become official. But more than 200 years later, our courts still use it.

Analysis: Score 3

*This paper is focused on the **topic** and has **order**. Vocabulary words delegates, framers, and convention are not enough to carry the point. Sentence patterns do not contribute to overall fluency, and details are sketchy. **Tone** is appropriate.*

Low

A bunch of men who have now been dead quite some time got together to discuss the fate of the country. They met in a stuffy meeting room in the summer with the windows boarded so their meeting could be private. They voted on it, signed it, and took it back to their own states.

Analysis: Score 2

This paper focuses on the topic, although it is not mentioned specifically in words. There is a beginning, middle, and end. However, words are not challenging or content based, sentence patterns are elementary level, details are nonexistent, and tone is too familiar for the task.

Writing Task: Write a brief summary of an historical event.

Student Samples: The Great Depression

1929 was an extremely grim time in the history of our country. The Great Depression brought devastation through loss of money, unemployment, and food shortages. The Great Depression had many causes, one being the uneven distribution of wealth and increased use of credit, especially in the purchase of stocks. Next was overproduction, where goods were produced but never sold. Finally, overspeculation (the overpricing of stocks) and too little money in circulation by the Federal Reserve were too much for the country to bear. Luckily, President Roosevelt's leadership brought the country out of this disastrous struggle.

Analysis: Score 6 *This paper focuses on the* ***topic****, is well* ***organized****, and uses content-based* ***vocabulary****: devastated, distribution, overproduction, over speculation, circulation, disastrous.* ***Sentence patterns*** *contribute to overall fluency,* ***details*** *are precise, and* ***tone*** *is appropriate.*

The stock market crash in 1929 caused the worst economic times in American history. It was called the Great Depression. During the depression there were labor strikes and famine throughout the entire country. Millions of people became unemployed and eventually homeless. Thankfully, after the 1932 election FDR's New Deal helped to put America back on its feet.

Analysis: Score 5 *This paper focuses on the* ***topic*** *and has* ***logical order****, but unimpressive vocabulary.* ***Sentence patterns*** *create fluency,* ***details*** *are provided, and the* ***tone*** *is appropriate.*

The stock market crash of 1929 caused many problems in our country. Caused by the Dow-Jones average hitting an all-time high, then plummeting down. Anyone who had money in banks lost it. Many lost jobs and couldn't provide for their families. Food was scarce. This event,The Great Depression, was one of the darkest in American History.

Analysis: Score 4 *The paper is* ***focused*** *and has* ***logical order****. Vocabulary is ordinary. Most sentence patterns are complex, but the fragment (second sentence) contributes too much to lack of fluency – so no point.* ***Details*** *support the topic, and* ***tone*** *is appropriate.*

The Great Depression was a great part of American history. It took place in the Great Plains. What caused the Great Depression was an uneven distribution of wealth and overspeculation. Overspectulation is the overpricing of stocks. This lead to the stock market crashing, which eventually shut down most of our great country. As you can clearly see, the Great Depression was a terrible event to the United States.

Analysis: Score 3 *This paper focuses on the **topic** and has basic **order**. Vocabulary is ordinary and the repeated use of "great" is noticeable. Sentence patterns are somewhat choppy with structural problems as well. Examples are given, but there are no details to support them. The **tone** is appropriate.*

The Great Depression was very depressing, overspeculation in the workplace is what caused it. People lost their life savings and were all poor after this point in time. People were not happy. They were sad and depressed. It was awful.

Analysis: Score 2 *This paper is written at a low level, but focuses on the topic and has an orderly structure. No other points are given.*

There was this one time when like this army or whatever won this war. It was like a crazy time because those people had never experienced something like it. It was an inspiration to all. Suddenly the Great Depression began.

Analysis: Score 1 *This is a meager attempt to focus on the topic. Little knowledge is shared about the Great Depression, other than mentioning it.*

Writing Across the Curriculum in FOREIGN LANGUAGE

Remember:

- Implementation of The Simple 6™ should be done in Language Arts classes.
- The students in your classes know the program. Let them help you.

When writing about FOREIGN LANGUAGE/CULTURES:

- Always use The Simple 6™ components. Call them by name.
- Refer to your classroom poster throughout the year.
- Focus on the development of the concise, content-based paragraph.
- Recognize the value in 10-15 minute opportunities to write: essay questions, reflections, critiques, opinions, etc.
- Set a monthly or quarterly goal *(personal or as per school improvement plan).*
- Score the writing using The Simple 6™ mini rubric.
- Analyze and turn in data.
- Model appropriate responses so students get a better understanding of the exemplary expectation.

IDEAS FOR WRITING ABOUT

FOREIGN LANGUAGE/ CULTURES

Describe a foreign tradition that is not seen in the United States.

Reflect on how difficult it is to become fluent in another language.

Persuade your parents to let you study for a semester in a foreign country, so you can become more fluent in speaking the language.

ADDITIONAL WRITING ACTIVITIES FOR FOREIGN LANGUAGE/CULTURES:

1.

2.

3.

A general weakness I see in writing about FOREIGN CULTURES is:

____

____

____

FOREIGN LANGUAGES

Name: ____________________
Date: ____________________
Class: ____________________

***WRITING TASK*: Describe a foreign tradition that is not seen in the United States.**

Write a concise paragraph that:

- introduces the topic
- provides specific cultural details
- uses precise terminology
- has a concluding statement

You may choose to write a paragraph that only contains five sentences.
Know, however, that your paragraph will be assessed on the following:

- *Did you focus on the assigned topic?*
- *Are your thoughts in order?*
- *Did you include challenging vocabulary?*
- *Did you vary sentence patterns to avoid a list-like paragraph?*
- *Did you provide exceptional supporting details?*
- *Is the tone of your writing appropriate for the task?*

Planning Space: Use the back of this page to plan your writing.

Writing in FOREIGN LANGUAGE/CULTURES

WRITING TASK: Describe a foreign tradition that is not seen in the U.S.

Student Samples: Unique Traditions

High

In the historically rich land of Israel, Jewish people have many traditions, especially at major life events such as weddings, funerals, and births. One interesting tradition that can be observed during a Jewish wedding is the breaking of the glass. The bride and groom stand under the canopy, which is like an arch or an arbor above their heads. The rabbi puts a glass on the floor, and instructs the groom to stomp on it (Yes, it sounds odd, but it's true!) When the groom's black shoe comes thundering down, the glass shatters, and everyone erupts in applause and celebratory cheers. This tradition symbolizes the end of the old, single life and the beginning of a new life of as husband and wife. It is exciting and dramatic, and also a good reason to keep your shoes on at a Jewish wedding reception!

Analysis: Score 6

*This paragraph focuses on the **topic**, has logical **order**, and uses content-based **vocabulary** words such as canopy, arch, arbor, erupts, celebratory, symbolizes. **Sentence patterns** contribute to overall fluency, **details** are descriptive, and **tone** is appropriate.*

Average

Japanese people respect and honor children in an unusual way. One day each year the Japanese celebrate "Boys' Day", and on a different day in a different month they celebrate "Girls' Day". Each of these days has a name in Japanese, but I can't remember them. Kids must love these special days because they enjoy many fun activities. They also get gifts and get a day off of school! Very cool!

Analysis: Score 3

*This paragraph focuses on the **topic**, has **order**, and provides some **details**. Although they are not exceptional, we understand the nature of the tradition. Vocabulary is ordinary, sentence structure is low level, and the tone is too familiar.*

Low

England is where they take a break for tea in the afternoon. It's a tradition there. We don't take a tea break here in the United States. We do have coffee breaks though. I don't think they have to drink tea if they don't like it.

Analysis: Score 1

*The paragraph **attempts** to focus on the **topic**, although not much information is provided. Order is weak, vocabulary is ordinary and sentence patterns are elementary level. Details do not specifically describe the tradition, and tone is too informal.*

FOREIGN LANGUAGES

Name: ____________________
Date: ____________________
Class: ____________________

WRITING TASK: ***Reflect on how difficult it is to become fluent in another language.***

Write a concise paragraph that:

- introduces the topic
- provides specific supporting details
- uses precise, cultural terminology
- has a concluding statement

You may choose to write a paragraph that only contains five sentences.
Know, however, that your paragraph will be assessed on the following:

- *Did you focus on the assigned topic?*
- *Are your thoughts in order?*
- *Did you include challenging, content-based vocabulary?*
- *Did you vary sentence patterns to avoid a list-like paragraph?*
- *Did you provide exceptional supporting details?*
- *Was the tone of your writing appropriate for the task?*

Planning Space: Use the back of this page to plan your writing.

Writing about FOREIGN CULTURES

WRITING TASK:* *Reflect on how difficult it is to become fluent in another language.

Student Samples: Reflections

On a scale of one to ten (ten being most difficult), I would have to rate learning a new language as an 8. Languages have so many unique characteristics like spelling patterns, dialects, cultural phrases, and similar words. For many, it is difficult to master those skills in their native tongue, let alone in another language! Another obstacle to being able to speak fluently can be embarrassment. Sometimes language students speak slowly because they don't want to say the wrong thing and sound ignorant or offensive, so they hold back. To build fluency, you must "go for it", saturating yourself with the language. You have to take risks, and practice constantly. Many people just don't make this a priority, and it negatively affects their fluency. If you can study in that country for a semester, that is definitely the best plan for becoming fluent in any language.

Analysis: Score 6

The paper focuses on the ***topic*** *and has logical* ***order****.* ***Vocabulary*** *words such as* dialects, cultural phrases, native tongue, *and* fluency *are above average.* ***Sentence patterns*** *are complex and* ***details*** *support the topic.* ***Tone*** *is appropriate.*

There are many reasons why it is difficult to become fluent in a foreign language, especially Spanish. First, you have to understand verbs and how they change. Second, it is easy to forget words, so you pause to try and recall how to say something. Third, getting the correct accent is tough because sometimes the sounds you need to make don't even exist in English. Lastly, the sentence structure in Spanish is different from English. The hardest thing about learning Spanish is that if you go to Mexico on vacation, and you think you will be able to practice, they speak so fast that it's almost impossible to understand. Then, if you ask a question nice and slowly in Spanish, they answer in Spanish at lightning speed - and you still don't know the answer! Learning to be fluent in a new language can be a huge challenge.

Analysis: Score 5

*This paragraph focuses on the **topic** and has logical **order**. Vocabulary is ordinary. **Sentence patterns** and **details** are sufficient, and **tone** is appropriate.*

Learning English has been a very hard task. It was hard to learn it before we came here from Mexico. When we got here, we had to start school right away. Everyone was speaking English and no one was speaking Spanish. As I learned English, it was still hard because everyone at home speaks only Spanish. I think it would be very helpful to have schools for people to learn just English and let the parents come too.

Analysis: Score 3

*This paragraph focuses on the **topic** and has **order**. Vocabulary is ordinary. Sentences are lower level but correct. Details are basic, but **tone** is appropriate.*

Learning English has been very hard for me and my sister. We try to listen to the teachers when we are at school. At home everyone speak Spanish. We can practice with our friends. It is not easy to learn language and school subjects at the same time.

Analysis: Score 3

*This student focuses on the **topic** and presents her ideas in **order**. Language is ordinary and details are low level. Sentence patterns are mostly correct but basic in structure. **Tone** is appropriate for the task.*

It is hard to learn another language, because there are so many words to know. You can't really read it to study, so it takes a long time.

Analysis: Score 1

*This students **attempts** to focus on the **topic**.*

Writing Across the Curriculum in PE/HEALTH

Remember:

- Implementation of The Simple 6™ should be done in Language Arts classes.
- The students in your classes know the program. Let them help you.

When writing about PE/HEALTH:

- Always use The Simple 6™ components. Call them by name.
- Refer to your classroom poster throughout the year.
- Focus on the development of the concise, content-based paragraph.
- Recognize the value in 10-15 minute opportunities to write: essay questions, reflections, critiques, opinions, etc.
- Set a monthly or quarterly goal *(personal or as per school improvement plan).*
- Score the writing using The Simple 6™ mini rubric.
- Analyze and turn in data.
- Model appropriate responses so students get a better understanding of the exemplary expectation.

IDEAS FOR WRITING ABOUT PE/HEALTH

Describe a healthy way to lose ten pounds.

Explain how to play. . .(any game).

Explain why it is important to exercise.

ADDITIONAL WRITING ACTIVITIES FOR PE/HEALTH:

1.

2.

3.

A general weakness I see in writing about PE/HEALTH is:

____

____

____

PE/HEALTH

Name: ____________________
Date: ____________________
Class: ____________________

WRITING TASK: Describe a healthy way to lose ten pounds.

Write a concise paragraph that:

- introduces the topic
- provides specific, content-based supporting details
- uses precise, health-related terminology
- has a concluding statement

You may choose to write a paragraph that only contains five sentences. Know, however, that your paragraph will be assessed on the following:

- *Did you focus on the assigned topic?*
- *Are your thoughts in order?*
- *Did you include challenging, health-related vocabulary?*
- *Did you vary sentence patterns to avoid a list-like paragraph?*
- *Did you provide exceptional supporting details?*
- *Is the tone of your writing appropriate for the task?*

Planning Space: Use the back of this page to plan your writing.

Writing in PE/Health

Writing Task: Describe a healthy way to lose ten pounds.

Student Samples: Weight Loss

High

Losing ten pounds is a task which many people would like to achieve, and it's actually not as hard as it seems. You'll just need drive, determination, and a good health plan that consists of eating right, exercise, and staying active. Healthy eating habits could begin by choosing a favorite fruit over a snack, and possibly eating more salads and healthier foods. Exercise simply means working to achieve a certain body figure, so you should exercise daily. Staying active is probably one of the easiest tasks, although many mistake it for exercise. Don't sit around watching TV. Get motivated, go outside and do something! If you stick with this easy plan you could lose ten pounds.

Analysis: Score 6

*This paragraph focuses on the **topic**, has logical **order**, and high level **vocabulary** words such as achieve, determination, motivated. **Sentence patterns** are complex, **details** are descriptive, and **tone** is appropriate.*

Average

There are thousands of ways that a person could possibly lose weight, but not every one of them is healthy though. Just stopping eating or making yourself throw up after you eat is not good for you at all. Three things that you can do is set goals, diet, and exercise. If you would do these things you would be surprised at how quickly you'll lose weight.

Analysis: Score 3

*This paragraph focuses on the **topic**, has **order**, and has an appropriate **tone**. Words, sentence patterns, and details are lower level.*

Low

There's a lot of ways to lose ten pounds. One way would be exercising about five times a day for about two hours. Another way would be go on a diet. Last thing you would probably be the best way would be doing tybo it doesent only tech you how to fight it helps you lose a lot of weight.

Analysis: Score 2

This paragraph focuses on the **topic** and **attempts** to provides some **details**. A conclusion is needed as are high level vocabulary words. Sentence structure is faulty, and tone is too informal.

PE/HEALTH

Name: ____________________
Date: ____________________
Class: ____________________

WRITING TASK: Write a brief summary that explains the game of basketball.

Write a concise paragraph that:

- introduces the topic
- provides specific supporting details
- uses precise, basketball-related terminology
- has a concluding statement

You may choose to write a paragraph that only contains five sentences. Know, however, that your paragraph will be assessed on the following:

- *Did you focus on the assigned topic?*
- *Are your thoughts in order?*
- *Did you include challenging, content-based vocabulary?*
- *Did you vary sentence patterns to avoid a list-like paragraph?*
- *Did you provide exceptional supporting details?*
- *Is the tone of your writing appropriate for the task?*

Planning Space: Use the back of this page to plan your writing.

Writing about PE

Writing task: Write a brief summary that explains the game of basketball.

Student Samples: Basketball

Basketball is a competitive team sport that is played with five members on each team. The object of the game is to earn points by shooting a basketball into a hoop that is about ten feet high. Players on each team play offensively and defensively, depending on which team has the ball. There are many rules, addressing infringements such as traveling, double dribbling, charging, and many others. Making a basket counts for one, two, or three points, depending on how far away the shooter is. The game is played in eight minute quarters, and the team with the most points, obviously, wins.

Analysis: Score 6

*This paragraph focuses on the **topic**, has logical **order**, and uses precise **vocabulary** such as offensively, defensively, infringements, traveling, double dribbling, and charging. **Sentence patterns** create fluency, and **details** are precise. **Tone** is appropriate for the task.*

Basketball is a team game played with five players on each team. The object is to shoot the ball into a basket that is ten feet above the ground. There are two point field goals, three point field goals, shot from beyond an arc a specified distance form the basket, and free throws worth one point. The team with the most total points is the winner. There are many rules that govern the game (rulebooks full to be exact) that must be learned prior to playing. Basketball is a great game because it is fast, exciting, and allows people of various sizes and talents to play.

Analysis: Score 5

*This paragraph focuses on the **topic** and has logical **order**. **Sentence patterns** contribute to fluency and **details** of the game are provided. **Tone** is appropriate, but vocabulary could be more specific and content-related.*

Have you ever played basketball? It is so fun! You get to pass top your teammates, dribble, and shoot an orange basketball into a hoop. If you travel or charge someone you could get a foul and the other team will get to shoot a free throw. The team who has the most points at the end of the game is the winner! Yea!

Analysis: Score 4

*This paragraph focuses on the **topic** and has **order**. Vocabulary is ordinary. **Sentence patterns** contribute to fluency and game **details** are provided. Tone is too informal.*

Basketball is a great team game. You dribble, shoot, and pass. It keeps you active, and you have to practice specific skills if you want to be a good player. Whichever team scores the most points wins the game, which has two halfs or sometimes quarters. You get points when the basketball goes threw the hoop. Mostly it's two, but you could also get one for free throws or three for a three-point shot. There are also fouls that you can get if you make certain kinds of mistakes during the game.

Analysis: Score 3

*This paragraph focuses on the **topic**. It does not have logical order because the conclusion is missing and sentences don't follow a prescribed sequence. Vocabulary is average. **Sentence patterns** are relatively fluent and **details** are provided. Because the writer used the word you so much, I felt the tone was too informal.*

In basketball you try to get a ball in the hoop. You get two points for each basket. There are two teams that play against each other. The team who gets the most points wins.

Analysis: Score 2

*This paragraph focuses on the **topic** and has logical **order**. Vocabulary, sentence patterns and details are average. It's difficult to determine the tone because sentence structure is so basic.*

It's fun. Dribbling is a part of it. You shoot the orange ball to get points. And you pass. You also play on a team.

Analysis: Score 1

*This paragraph provides **limited details**, but we don't really know the topic because it is never mentioned. Vocabulary and sentence patterns are low level. Tone is too informal.*

Writing Across the Curriculum in BUSINESS

Remember:

- Implementation of The Simple 6™ should be done in Language Arts classes.
- The students in your classes know the program. Let them help you.

When writing about BUSINESS:

- Always use The Simple 6™ components. Call them by name.
- Refer to your classroom poster throughout the year.
- Focus on the development of the concise, content-based paragraph.
- Recognize the value in 10-15 minute opportunities to write: essay questions, reflections, critiques, opinions, etc.
- Set a monthly or quarterly goal *(personal or as per school improvement plan).*
- Score the writing using The Simple 6™ mini rubric.
- Analyze and turn in data.
- Model appropriate responses so students get a better understanding of the exemplary expectation.

IDEAS FOR WRITING ABOUT **BUSINESS**

Explain how finance relates to everyday life.

Describe how technology has affected the business world.

Imagine you have employees. Describe your management style.

ADDITIONAL WRITING ACTIVITIES FOR BUSINESS:

1.

2.

3.

A general weakness I see in writing about BUSINESS is:

____

____

____

BUSINESS

Name: ____________________
Date: ____________________
Class: ____________________

WRITING TASK: Explain how finance relates to everyday life.

Write a concise paragraph that:

- introduces the topic
- provides specific, content-based supporting details
- uses precise finance-related terminology
- has a concluding statement

You may choose to write a paragraph that only contains five sentences.
Know, however, that your paragraph will be assessed on the following:

- *Did you focus on the assigned topic?*
- *Are your thoughts in order?*
- *Did you include challenging vocabulary?*
- *Did you vary sentence patterns to avoid a list-like paragraph?*
- *Did you provide exceptional, business-oriented, supporting details?*
- *Is the tone of your writing appropriate for the task?*

Planning Space: Use the back of this page to plan your writing.

Writing about BUSINESS

Writing Task: Explain how finance relates to everyday life.

Student Samples: Everyday Finances

High

Finance has to do with money, and money is a part of daily life. Investments such as stocks, bonds, money market accounts and CD's help adults plan for their future. Lending institutions like mortgage companies, banks, and credit unions help people to get loans for new homes, vehicles, and other things. Credit cards lend money to people for everything from lunch at McDonald's to a new pair of designer jeans. It's amazing that more classes aren't offered in finance, because most ordinary people really need advice on this subject.

Analysis: Score 6

*This paragraph focuses on the **topic**, has logical **order**, and uses precise **vocabulary** for the subject such as investments, stocks, bonds, money market accounts, lending institutions, and mortgage companies. **Sentence patterns** create fluency, **details** are descriptive and precise, and **tone** is appropriate.*

Average

Learning how to handle your money is very important. Balancing your check book, paying your bills, and not getting too much credit card debt will help you to keep your finances in order. You will probably need to learn how to make a budget. This will keep you from spending more than you have. Finance definitely relates to our everyday lives.

Analysis: Score 3

*This paragraph focuses on the **topic** and has logical **order**. Vocabulary is unimpressive. **Sentence patterns** help to create fluency, but details are sketchy. Tone could go either way. This could be either a 3 or a 4.*

Low

Get your finance in order or you might have to go bankrupted. You will lose everything. So don't charge too much stuff.

Analysis: Score 1

*An **attempt** is made to focus on the **topic.***

BUSINESS

Name: ____________________
Date: ____________________
Class: ____________________

WRITING TASK: Explain how technology has changed the business world.

Write a concise paragraph that:

- introduces the topic
- provides specific, content-based supporting details
- uses precise, technological terminology
- has a concluding statement

You may choose to write a paragraph that only contains five sentences.
Know, however, that your paragraph will be assessed on the following:

- *Did you focus on the assigned topic?*
- *Are your thoughts in order?*
- *Did you include business vocabulary?*
- *Did you vary sentence patterns to avoid a list-like paragraph?*
- *Did you provide exceptional, business-oriented, supporting details?*
- *Was the tone of your writing appropriate for the task?*

Planning Space: Use the back of this page to plan your writing.

Writing about BUSINESS

Writing Task: Explain how technology has changed the business world.

Student Samples: Technology in Business

Do you realize how vital a role technology plays in the business world today? Financial transactions like investments or money transfers can be completed on your own computer. Scanners and self-checkout lanes make paying for items quick and error free. Communication systems such as cell phones, email, and text messaging allow people in business to communicate immediately. Navigation systems automatically guide people in sales to unknown locations, while telecommunicating allows them to travel less. Technology is not only changing the business world; it has become the backbone of business itself in this century.

Analysis: Score 6

This paragraph focuses on the ***topic****, has logical* ***order****, and uses precise* ***vocabulary*** *such as* financial transactions, investments, scanners, communication systems, *and* telecommunicating. ***Sentence patterns*** *create overall fluency, and* ***details*** *are precise.* ***Tone*** *is appropriate for the task.*

The most dramatic change in the business world has been its forward move in terms of communication. It started with a monstrous cell phone that was geared toward emergency road service and ambulance drivers. Phone size decreased and Palm Pilots, with a daily planner and an address book included, became available as a separate device. Then came laptop and notebook computers, e-mail, video conferencing, digital photography, and text messaging. Now combined into one miniscule device that weighs less than a pound, these advances in technology have changed the business world in terms of simplicity, accuracy, and speed.

Analysis: Score 6

This paper focuses on the ***topic****, has logical* ***order****, and uses higher level as well as content-related* ***vocabulary****. (dramatic, communication, Palm Pilots, device, laptop, video-conferencing, and miniscule)* ***Sentence patterns*** *contribute to overall fluency,* ***details*** *are precise, and* ***tone*** *is appropriate for the task.*

The business world would be nothing without many of the new technological devices we have today. Computers make everything faster and easier, cellphones make it easier to contact others, and laptops allow you to take your work anywhere. Before technology, everything was done manually. Research was done in libraries, orders were called in or mailed, and bank business was done at the bank. This took a lot of time. Technology makes everything instantaneous, usually with fewer errors. The impact technology has made on the business world is indescribable.

Analysis: Score 5

This paper focuses on the ***topic****, has logical* ***order****, and uses precise* ***vocabulary*** *such as* technological devices, manually, instantaneous, *and* impact. ***Sentence patterns*** *create fluency; details are satisfactory but could be more precise.* ***Tone*** *is appropriate.*

The advancements in technology over the years has done great things for business. Those advancements range from e-mail to being able to jump on a jet plane to get to a meeting. Have you ever thought about how long it used to take to snail mail everything? Technology is the best thing to ever happen to the business world.

Analysis: Score 3

This paragraph focuses on the ***topic****, has logical* ***order****, and* ***sentence patterns*** *that are satisfactory. Vocabulary is ordinary, details are unimpressive, and tone is too informal.*

Business is affected year round with new technology inventions. Factories, transportation, and so much more is involved with technology. Even schools rely on technology use. So many things rely on technology that it's a vital need for every day use.

Analysis: Score 2

This paper receives a point for focusing on the ***topic*** *and* ***attempting*** *to provide exceptional supporting* ***details****.*

How would technology have changed for the business world. It has changed a lot over the years because all the new technology has changed. All the new technology we have is all up to date. We have a lot of new computer software too.

Analysis: Score 1

The question here is whether to give the point for focusing on the topic even though he strayed at the end, or take the point away from logical order because of a faulty conclusion. One point was given for ***attempting*** *to focus on the* ***topic****.*

A long time ago there really wasn't a lot of technology, but now everything we do we have to use some kind of new technology.

Analysis: Score 1

This paper receives one point for focusing on the ***topic****.*

Writing Across the Curriculum in FINE ARTS

Remember:
- Implementation of The Simple 6™ should be done in Language Arts classes.
- The students in your classes know the program. Let them help you.

When writing about the FINE ARTS:
- Always use The Simple 6™ components. Call them by name.
- Refer to your classroom poster throughout the year.
- Focus on the development of the concise, content-based paragraph.
- Recognize the value in 10-15 minute opportunities to write: essay questions, reflections, critiques, opinions, etc.
- Set a monthly or quarterly goal *(personal or as per school improvement plan).*
- Score the writing using The Simple 6™ mini rubric.
- Analyze and turn in data.
- Model appropriate responses so students get a better understanding of the exemplary expectation.

IDEAS FOR WRITING ABOUT FINE ARTS

Describe the style of a famous artist or musician.

Explain why a certain artist or musician is your favorite.

Reflect on how certain types of music or art make you feel.

ADDITIONAL WRITING ACTIVITIES FOR THE FINE ARTS:

1.

2.

3.

A general weakness I see in writing about the FINE ARTS is:

____

____

____

FINE ARTS

Name: ____________________
Date: ____________________
Class: ____________________

WRITING TASK: Describe the style of Pablo Picasso.

Write a concise paragraph that:

- introduces the topic
- provides specific, content-based details
- uses artistic terms and other related vocabulary
- has a concluding statement

You may choose to write a paragraph that only contains five sentences.
Know, however, that your paragraph will be assessed on the following:

- *Did you focus on the assigned topic?*
- *Are your thoughts in order?*
- *Did you include precise vocabulary?*
- *Did you vary sentence patterns to avoid a list-like paragraph?*
- *Did you provide exceptional supporting details?*
- *Is the tone of your writing appropriate for the task?*

Planning Space: Use the back of this page to plan your writing.

Writing about Art

Writing Task: Describe the style of (choice of artist).

Student Samples: The Work of Pablo Picasso

High

Pablo Picasso, born in 1881 in Malaga, Spain, was one of the most unique artists of the twentieth century. His artistic expression on canvas progressed throughout the stages of his life. He identified these stages himself, with names like his "Blue Period", "Rose Period", and the turning point of his career, "Cubism". Other than his sculptures and ceramics, Picasso's artistic medium was oil on canvas. From his early, more realistic works such as "Girl in a Chemise", to the surrealism of "Woman with a Flower", and finally to the sadness and horror of "Guernica", Picasso will always be remembered as the artist who painted with passion, never caring about or encouraging public interpretation.

Analysis: Score 6

*This paragraph focuses on the **topic**, has logical **order**, and uses content-based **vocabulary** such as* cubism, artist medium, surrealism, *and* interpretation. ***Sentences** are rather long but contribute to fluency. **Details** are precise and **tone** is appropriate.*

Average

Picasso is famous because his work was so abstract. He always painted oil on canvas and his paintings were very unusual. People didn't understand them. Picasso didn't really care. He didn't think people needed to understand every painting. He thought they should just enjoy his work. Some examples are "The Violin", "Man with Guitar", and "Weeping Woman". His work will always stand out because it is so weird.

Analysis: Score 3

*This paragraph focuses on the **topic** and has **order**. Other than abstract, vocabulary is not challenging or content-based. Sentence patterns are similar in structure. Details are provided, but they are not exceptional. Tone is satisfactory, but not definite. I would give a **half point to supporting details** and **half point for the audience connection**.*

Low

Picasso's style was weird. He took people's heads and body parts and broke them into pieces. Then he put them back in strange ways. He used mostly a lot of color, but during his Blue period he used mostly blue. His paints are very hard to understand.

Analysis: Score 2

*This paper focuses on the **topic** and **attempts** to provide supporting **details**.*

FINE ARTS

Name: ____________________
Date: ____________________
Class: ____________________

WRITING TASK: Describe why a musician or musical group is your favorite.

Write a concise paragraph that:

- introduces the topic
- provides specific details
- uses musical terms and other related vocabulary
- has a concluding statement

You may choose to write a paragraph that only contains five sentences. Know, however, that your paragraph will be assessed on the following:

- *Did you focus on the assigned topic?*
- *Are your thoughts in order?*
- *Did you include precise, content-based vocabulary?*
- *Did you vary sentence patterns to avoid a list-like paragraph?*
- *Did you provide exceptional supporting details?*
- *Is the tone of your writing appropriate for the task?*

Planning Space: Use the back of this page to plan your writing.

Writing about Music

Writing Task: Explain why a musician or musical group is your favorite.

Student Samples: My Favorite Group

My favorite musical artist is Iron and Wine. I love absolutely everything they do. The songs are so meaningful that sometimes I get the lyrics stuck in my head for days. All of their musical themes are extremely sad, serious, or haunting and have deep meanings. The lyrics inspire you to reflect on your own life. You might hear their music in the background of a coffee shop but it is also regularly featured on "Grey's Anatomy". Personally, I have their music playing on my Myspace page. I think they are a really talented group and if I wrote music, that's definitely the style I would try to achieve. The acoustic guitar paired with the vocals make it unique and inspirational. That's why I like Iron and Wine.

Analysis: Score 6

This paragraph focuses on the ***topic****, has logical* ***order****, and* ***vocabulary*** *words such as* lyrics, musical themes, featured, achieve, acoustic, *and* inspirational. ***Sentence patterns*** *contribute to overall fluency, and* ***details*** *are mostly reflective but appropriate.* ***Tone*** *may be construed as too informal, but it works for the style of the writing.*

One of my favorite musicians would definitely be John Legend, who was born in Ohio. His smooth vocals go nicely over the chill, mellow R and B production used in his songs. His music is very traditional and appeals to many people of all ages. His career as a professional artist has been short, but he has released two great albums (the latter of the two being my favorite). I would definitely recommend that you check him out if you haven't already.

Analysis: Score 5

This paragraph focuses on the ***topic****, has logical* ***order****, fluent* ***sentence patterns****, and descriptive* ***details****.* ***Tone*** *is appropriate, but vocabulary is limited.*

I really like Jack Johnson. His music has a really mellow style that reminds me of the beach. It sounds like music you would hear a guy playing on the beach in Hawaii. He's kind of a hipee. He is barefoot in a lot of his shows. He has a lot of good lyrics too. Many of them are about keeping life simple and not being into material things. I like the one that says "Look at all those fancy clothes…but these can keep us warm just like those….what about your soul, is it ready to be sold?" He always makes songs that remind you what life should be about. His music always puts me in a good mood, and I think that's why I like it. He is good friends with another artist who I really like named Ben Harper. Sometimes they go on tour together and the concerts are awesome. If you have never heard of one of these guys, you should check them out sometime. If you like kicking back and relaxing, you'd probably like them a lot.

Analysis: Score 4

*This paper focuses on the **topic**, but struggles with logical order. Vocabulary is not content-based. **Sentence patterns** create fluency and **details** are provided. The **tone** is appropriate for the total piece, but more formality may be expected. This point could go either way.*

My favorite group is Daft Punk. They have a british techno rhythm. The coolest part about them is that all their music and voices are computer generated! The fact that its all generated is lost within the lifelike sounds that Daft Punk outputs. That is why they are my favorite.

Analysis: Score 3

*This paper immediately receives points for focusing on the **topic**, and having logical **order**. Vocabulary to consider would be techno rhythm, computer generated, and outputs. Sentence patterns are definitely list-like. Supporting details are provided, but they are far from exceptional, so I will give a **half point to vocabulary** and a **half point to details**, something I try to avoid. The audience connection is not focused on providing information.*

My favorite music group is G-Unit. I like the group G-Unit because they make very good music and the feeling of the music is very positive. G-Unit also has the best rapper, known as 50 Cent. He is the owner of G-Unit.

Analysis: Score 1 or 2

*A point is given for focusing on the **topic** and an **attempt** point may or may not be given for providing **minimal details.***

My favorite music grop is Sublime because I like the beat and the sound. that is all I have to say about this

Analysis: Score 1

*This paper illustrates a meager **attempt** at focusing on the **topic**.*

Writing Across the Curriculum in FACS

Remember:

- Implementation of The Simple 6™ should be done in Language Arts classes.
- The students in your classes know the program. Let them help you.

When writing about FAMILY AND CONSUMER SCIENCE:

- Always use The Simple 6™ components. Call them by name.
- Refer to your classroom poster throughout the year.
- Focus on the development of the concise, content-based paragraph.
- Recognize the value in 10-15 minute opportunities to write: essay questions, reflections, critiques, opinions, etc.
- Set a monthly or quarterly goal *(personal or as per school improvement plan).*
- Score the writing using The Simple 6™ mini rubric.
- Analyze and turn in data.
- Model appropriate responses so students get a better understanding of the exemplary expectation.

IDEAS FOR WRITING ABOUT FAMILY AND CONSUMER SCIENCE

Describe how to make a favorite recipe.
Explain the importance of good nutrition.
Describe how your responsibilities will change when you have a child to care for.

ADDITIONAL WRITING ACTIVITIES FOR FACS:

1.

2.

3.

A general weakness I see in writing about FACS is:

____

____

____

FACS

Name: ____________________
Date: ____________________
Class: ____________________

WRITING TASK: Write a concise paragraph that describes how to make your favorite recipe.

Write a concise paragraph that:

- introduces the topic
- provides specific instructions
- uses vocabulary for cooking
- has a concluding statement

You may choose to write a paragraph that only contains five sentences. Know, however, that your paragraph will be assessed on the following:

- *Did you focus on the assigned topic?*
- *Are your thoughts in order?*
- *Did you include specific, recipe-related vocabulary?*
- *Did you vary sentence patterns to avoid a list-like paragraph?*
- *Did you provide exceptional supporting details and instructions?*
- *Is your tone appropriate for the task?*

Planning Space: Use the back of this page to plan your writing.

Writing about FAMILY AND CONSUMER SCIENCE

Writing Task:* *Write a concise paragraph that describes how to make your favorite recipe.

Student Samples: My Favorite Recipe

High

I love to make chocolate chunk cookies. Even though you can buy the dough in stores now, my grandma's recipe is definitely the most scrumptious! First, read the directions and turn the oven to 350 degrees. Next, place the ingredients and other supplies you will need on a clean workspace. Mix everything thoroughly in a large bowl (dry ingredients first), and spoon the dough onto the ungreased pans. Carefully put the pans in the oven for about 14 minutes. Then enjoy!

Analysis: Score 4

*This paper focuses on the **topic** and has logical **order**. Vocabulary such as scrumptious, ingredients, workspace, ungreased are noted but not outstanding. **Sentence patterns** contribute to fluency. Details are provided, but not precise, so **half point for vocabulary** and **half point for details**. The tone is more conversational than instructional.*

Average

My mom's spaghetti recipe from her Italian grandma is the best. Here's what to do. Put the tomatoes, secret spices, and other things into the sauce. It needs to cook for several hours. Then put the beef, veal, and other stuff together for the meatballs. The pasta gets cooked last so it won't be too mushy. Serve the meatballs first, and then bring out the pasta with hot garlic bread.

Analysis: Score 3

*This paragraph focuses on the **topic** and has logical **order**. Vocabulary is lacking. **Sentence patterns** create fluency, although their level is somewhat low. Details are not exceptional, and tone is too familiar.*

Low

My favorite recipe is brownies. Put the mix in the bowl with the egg and water. Cook it until it is done then eat them.

Analysis: Score 2

*This paragraph focuses on the **topic** and makes an **attempt** at logical **order** (or details). Either way, only 2 points are given.*

FACS

Name: ____________________
Date: ____________________
Class: ____________________

WRITING TASK: Why is it important to have good nutrition?

Write a concise paragraph that:

- introduces the topic
- provides specific instructions
- uses vocabulary for cooking
- has a concluding statement

You may choose to write a paragraph that only contains five sentences.
Know, however, that your paragraph will be assessed on the following:

- *Did you focus on the assigned topic?*
- *Are your thoughts in order?*
- *Did you include specific, recipe-related vocabulary?*
- *Did you vary sentence patterns to avoid a list-like paragraph?*
- *Did you provide exceptional supporting details and instructions?*
- *Is your tone appropriate for the task?*

Planning Space: Use the back of this page to plan your writing.

Writing about FAMILY AND CONSUMER SCIENCE

Writing Task: Why is it important to have good nutrition?

Student Samples: The Importance of Good Nutrition

Nutrition is important because it includes all the things your body needs to function and stay healthy. Good nutrition involves getting all the nutrients, such as carbs, fats, proteins, minerals, fiber, and vitamins into your digestive system. And don't forget about the importance of water intake. Flushing toxins is critical to a healthy body! So if you want to live longer and avoid health problems such as stroke, system failure, and heart disease, eat healthy!

Analysis: Score 6

*This paper focuses on the **topic**, has logical **order**, and uses **vocabulary** words such as function, nutrients, carbs, fiber, digestive, and toxins. **Sentence patterns** create fluency, **details** are provided, and **tone** is appropriate.*

The importance of nutrition can't be stressed enough if a person wants to stay strong and healthy. Nutritionally speaking, two main factors to consider would be diet and exercise. Making smart food choices is something you want to seriously think about every time you open your mouth. You can't expect to eat junk food and stay healthy. Exercising every day, even just walking, will improve the way you feel. If you don't have good nutrition your life might end before you want it to, so make good nutrition a part of your life.

Analysis: Score 5

*This paper focuses on the **topic** and has logical **order**. Vocabulary is basic. **Sentence patterns** create fluency, **details** are provided although they could be more specific, and **tone** is appropriate.*

If you don't have good nutrition, then you must have bad nutrition. Which means your teeth could be messed up, arteries clogged up, heart attacks, and everything else. You've gotta eat all of the right things. Sometimes you can eat that whole pizza or that cake, but eat a salad sometimes also. You should try to have good nutrition every day.

Analysis: Score 3
*This paper focuses on the **topic** and is generally organized. Vocabulary is basic and sentence structure needs improvement. Some **details** and examples are provided, but the tone should be more informational.*

It's important to keep your nutrients in you because if you don't have it you could have weight loss, eating disorders, overall health, heart problems and many more. Nutrient is also important because you couldn't live without it. You need nutrients to keep your body moving and functioning. Also your body needs to stay functional or you could become very ill or something like that.

Analysis: Score 3
*This paragraph focuses on the **topic** and has a basic **order**. Vocabulary could go either way with weight loss, eating disorders, and functional. Sentences are basic with several problems in structure. Details are provided, but they are not specific. Because of that, I'd give a **half point to vocabulary** and a **half point to details**. Tone is too informal and confusing.*

Good nutrition is very important because if you don't have it you could get over weight or under it. You may not be sick all that much. You'd have more energy to do stuff. You should always eat the right foods.

Analysis: Score 2
*This paragraph focuses on the **topic** and has **order**. Vocabulary is basic, sentence structure is low level, details are not precise, and tone is lacking.*

So you can stay healty. So you don't die at a young age. Espaisaly if you have a wife and children you don't want to leave them do you. You also need it to keep good weight

Analysis: Score 1
*An **attempt** is made to focus on the **topic**.*

Writing Across the Curriculum in INDUSTRIAL TECH

Remember:

- Implementation of The Simple 6™ should be done in Language Arts classes.
- The students in your classes know the program. Let them help you.

When writing about INDUSTRIAL TECHNOLOGY:

- Always use The Simple 6™ components. Call them by name.
- Refer to your classroom poster throughout the year.
- Focus on the development of the concise, content-based paragraph.
- Recognize the value in 10-15 minute opportunities to write: essay questions, reflections, critiques, opinions, etc.
- Set a monthly or quarterly goal *(personal or as per school improvement plan).*
- Score the writing using The Simple 6™ mini rubric.
- Analyze and turn in data.
- Model appropriate responses so students get a better understanding of the exemplary expectation.

IDEAS FOR WRITING ABOUT INDUSTRIAL TECHNOLOGY

Describe the safety factors to be considered when using power tools.

Summarize what you have learned about building a house.

Explain how to measure for carpeting.

ADDITIONAL WRITING ACTIVITIES FOR INDUSTRIAL TECH:

1.

2.

3.

A general weakness I see in writing about INDUSTRIAL TECH is:

____

____

____

INDUSTRIAL TECHNOLOGY

Name: ______________________
Date: ______________________
Class: ______________________

WRITING TASK: Describe the safety factors to be considered when using power tools.

Write a concise paragraph that:

- introduces the topic
- provides specific, content-based details about safety.
- uses some of the terms of the trade
- has a concluding statement

You may choose to write a paragraph that only contains five sentences.
Know, however, that your paragraph will be assessed on the following:

- *Did you focus on the assigned topic?*
- *Are your thoughts in order?*
- *Did you include challenging vocabulary?*
- *Did you vary sentence patterns to avoid a list-like paragraph?*
- *Did you provide exceptional supporting details?*
- *Is the tone of your writing appropriate for the task?*

Planning Space: Use the back of this page to plan your writing.

Writing in INDUSTRIAL TECHNOLOGY

Writing Task: Describe the safety factors to be considered when using power tools.

Student Samples: Power Tool Safety

High

There are many safety issues to keep in mind if you are using power tools for the first time. First of all you should be wearing appropriate clothes that will not get caught in the equipment, removing jewelry that hangs down, and tying back your hair if it is too long. Also, make sure that you are using the tool in a clean environment where there are no wet spots or flammable materials, or other things to get caught on. Is the tool working properly? Check it out first, reading over the owner's manual or looking at the diagrams if you aren't sure how to use it. If a problem does occur, get assistance immediately!

Analysis: Score 6

*This paper focuses on the **topic** of safety, has logical **order** and uses **vocabulary** such as* appropriate, equipment, environment, flammable, manual, diagram, *and* assistance. ***Sentence patterns** create fluency, several **details** and examples are given, and the **tone** is appropriate for the task.*

Average

Be careful when you use power tools, especially if it's your first time. Ask yourself if you know how to use the tool. Don't just guess, it might cut your finger off! Make sure there isn't a lot of clutter where you are working. You could slip and fall or drop the tool and break it! Lastly, use common sense and you should be OK.

Analysis: Score 3

*This paragraph focuses on the **topic** and has logical **order**. Vocabulary is basic, but **sentence structure** creates fluency. Details need to be more specific and tone should be more informational.*

Low

You have to be careful when you use power tools. You could get your clothes caught in it. Or slip on the wet floor. Walk slowly. Be careful when you use them. It could be a big mess!

Analysis: Score 2

*This paper focuses on the **topic** and has a basic **order**. Vocabulary is basic, and sentence patterns are low level. Details are lacking and tone is too familiar.*

INDUSTRIAL TECHNOLOGY

Name: ______________________
Date: ______________________
Class: ______________________

WRITING TASK: Summarize what you learned from the guest speaker about building your own house.

Write a concise paragraph that:

- introduces the topic
- provides specific, content-based details about safety.
- uses some of the terms of the trade
- has a concluding statement

You may choose to write a paragraph that only contains five sentences. Know, however, that your paragraph will be assessed on the following:

- *Did you focus on the assigned topic?*
- *Are your thoughts in order?*
- *Did you include challenging vocabulary?*
- *Did you vary sentence patterns to avoid a list-like paragraph?*
- *Did you provide exceptional supporting details?*
- *Is the tone of your writing appropriate for the task?*

Planning Space: Use the back of this page to plan your writing.

Writing about INDUSTRIAL TECHNOLOGY

Writing Task: ***Today in class, a guest speaker talked to you about how to design and build your own house. Summarize what you learned about building your own house.***

Student Samples: Building Your Own House

Today I learned about the process of building a house and the realization of how hard it is! You really have to have all your plans and thoughts together long before you start. Hand-drawn blue prints have to be computerized, materials such as trusses, studs, fascia, soffett, and insulation have to be ordered, and subcontractors have to be scheduled. And don't forget about going to the bank and getting all your loans and finances in order so you can pay for it! I definitely want to try this in the future.

Analysis: Score 6

*This paper focuses on the **topic**, has logical **order**, and uses **vocabulary** words of the trade such as trusses, fascia, soffett, and subcontractors. **Sentence patterns** create fluency, **details** are given, and the **tone** is appropriate for the task.*

While learning about building your own house today, I realized that I would really like to do this! Paying attention to detail, especially in regard to decorating, would most likely be my main responsibility, but I would love to be involved! The hard labor would probably be left to the subcontractors or my husband, as well as ordering all the supplies and making sure we passed all the inspections. I would really enjoy organizing the project, figuring out the details, and solving problems along the way. The sentimental value will be tremendous!

Analysis: Score 5

*This paper focuses on the **topic**, has logical **order**, and uses **vocabulary** of the trade such as* attention to detail, subcontractors, *and* inspections. ***Sentence patterns** contribute to fluency, and details are provided, although they could be more specific. Tone is right on the edge between being too informal. Because of this I would give a **half point to details** and a **half point to audience**.*

Learning about building your own house is a very important topic that should help kids with their future. I learned so much today that I would never have even thought about! Meeting everyone's individual needs by customizing your own house and going through the whole procedure with your family would be awesome!

Analysis: Score 3

This paragraph focuses on the ***topic*** *and has logical* ***order****. Vocabulary is basic, but* ***sentence structure*** *creates fluency. Specific, content-based details are avoided, and tone is too familiar.*

I learned that building a house is a lot of work. It takes planning, time, effort, and money. I also learned that you do a lot of math with planning and building a house. I doubt that I would ever build a house, but it does sound like an interesting project.

Analysis: Score 3

The paragraph focuses on the ***topic*** *and has logical* ***order****. Vocabulary is basic.* ***Sentence patterns*** *and* ***details*** *are satisfactory but not outstanding. For this reason I would give a* ***half point to each****. Tone is too familiar.*

I believe that one day maybe I would build my own house. I really don't believe I would have the patients to build it. It seems like it would take a long time. I don't think I'll be building my own home, but hey, you never know.

Analysis: Score 2

This paragraph focuses on the ***topic*** *and has logical* ***order****. Vocabulary is basic, sentence patterns do not contribute to the overall fluency of the piece. Details are lacking and the tone is too familiar.*

Today I learned about how to build a house. I learned how to get started and I really am now thinking about building my own house after I finish school I'm going to graduate doing x-ray tech/ultra-sounds. I think that would be fun. I like how you get to do it your way or the high way. I'm going to have to marry a construction worker. The house was very nice.

Analysis: Score 1

This paragraph ***attempts*** *to focus on the* ***topic****, even though she flits from subject to subject.*

Conclusion

The contributions of content-based teachers have a tremendous influence on overall growth in student writing skills. There are so many advantages to writing across the curriculum. Some reasons might include:

- *consistent and regular opportunities for students to write*
- *instruction based on content writing*
- *practice with a more informational tone*
- *school improvement effort that involves all staff members*
- *students realizing that writing is valued in all subject areas*

Reminders:

1) *Know how many content-based writing assessments have been designated by your school improvement plan.*

2. *Integrate writing into your current long-range planning.*

3) *Share exemplary responses so students have a clearer idea of the expectations.*

4) *Know when data reports are due and plan the task and scoring accordingly.*

5) *If a regular assignment is being used, tell students in advance that the quality of writing will also be asse4ssed.*

6) *Use the mini rubric for scoring.*

7) *Complete the Class Analysis Chart to document weaknesses that will drive future instruction.*

8) *Fill out the Quarterly Tracking Chart for Cross-curricular Writing to evaluate instructional effectiveness and to track student progress for accreditation or the school improvement plan.*

Chapter 5: Data-driven Instruction and Accountability

Your school improvement plan is complete. Goals have been selected based on standardized and local data, and strategies have been designed to help students meet those goals. The priority now for classroom teachers is to integrate the strategies into their standards-based lesson plans throughout the entire school year. In doing this, several things need to be taken into consideration: management, assessment tools, data analysis, classroom follow up, data collection and reporting, instructional leadership, and teacher accountability.

Task Management

Writing has obviously been selected as one of your school improvement goals. Receiving staff development training and putting The Simple 6™ into practice is the strategy. As a classroom teacher, what have you been asked to do in terms of putting the program in place? If you are an English teacher, you will be implementing the program with students over a six or nine week period. You will be required to periodically assess students to see if they have mastered the skills taught. As a content-area teacher you may be required to give short, periodic assessments based on your content. You may also be responsible for administering and scoring a formal prompt assessment. There are management issues to consider in both scenarios.

Time

How long a time is needed to accomplish the task? ______________________________

How often will assessment occur? ____

Where will you fit this into your schedule? ____

How often are you required to turn in data? to whom? _____________________________

Resources

Product

Once the task is completed, where are the samples going?

____

____

How will students get feedback on the task?

____

____

At the end of the year, how are the samples being organized for documentation?

____

____

Tools

Do you have copies of the mini rubric cut out and ready to use?

____

Do you have Class Analysis Charts ready to use?

____

The following pages show examples of completed mini rubrics and a partial Class Analysis Chart.

Assessment Tools that Directly Impact Instruction

Mini Rubric
(p. 81)

In this Score 4 paper, the student focused on the topic, had order that included an introduction and conclusion, used at least 3 higher level (or content based) vocabulary words, and included exceptional supporting details. However, sentence patterns did not impact the fluency of the writing - making it choppy and list-like. No attempt was made to connect with the audience (or in a content-based piece, the writing was too information or conversational).

The Simple 6™:
A Writing Rubric
for Secondary Students

0/1

__1__ Topic
__1__ Logical Order
__1__ Challenging Vocabulary
_____ Sentence Patterns
__1__ Exceptional Details
_____ Audience

__4__ TOTAL 4

If this score were being turned in as documentation for your school improvement plan, the student would receive 4/6 for content (explanation above) and 4/4 on conventions, because there were no obvious errors in spelling, capitalization, punctuation, or sentence/paragraph structure that impacted the flow of communication. Based on your school's grading scale, the student received a grade book score of 86% for content, and 88% for conventions (4 errors x 3 pts. = 12 pts. taken from 100%)

Class Analysis Chart

TASK: ______________________________ DATE _______

NAMES	TOPIC	ORDER	VOCAB	PATTERNS	DETAILS	AUDIENCE	TOTAL
Adams, Joe	1	1			1		3
Barker, Susan	1	1			1		3
Brennon, Jessica	1	1		1	1		4
Carter, Kelly	1	1		1	1	1	5
Champness, Ali	1	1	1			1	4
Danks, David	1	1		1	1		4
Davis, Darren	1	1			1		3

The purpose of the Class Analysis Chart is to look for overall weaknesses in skill so you can easily identify skills to reteach.

Secondary Class Analysis Chart

TASK: Favorite Person – Baseline **DATE** 8-15-07

NAMES	TOPIC	ORDER	VOCAB	PATTERNS	DETAILS	AUDIENCE	TOTAL	
Barnett	1	1			1		3	
Barns	1	att. 1					2	frag.
Bogart	1	1	1		1		4	
Chamberlin	1	1	1	1		1	5	
Danaher	1	1			1		3	¶
Gonzales	1	conc.			att. 1		2	sp.
Hannon	1	1	1	1			4	
Hartley	1	1	1	1	1		5	
Lazaridis	1	1		1			3	✓
Marczenko	1	1			1		3	
Naragon	1	1	1	1		1	5	
O'Hara	1	1		1	1		4	
Papaleo	1	1			1		3	¶
Rodriguez	1	1			1		3	
Roggeman	Own	topic					0	
Salaiz	1	att. 1					2	sp.
Saros	1	1	1	1		1	5	
Scheu	1	1	1		1		4	
Soule	1	1		1	1		4	
Szuba	1	1	1/2		1/2		3	
Trkulja	Own	topic					0	
Varda	1	1	1		1		4	
Weaver	1	conc.		1			2	
Weber	1	1	1	1	1	1	6	
Zbrzezny	1	conc.	1	1			3	✓

Comments / Reflection:

Focus on the prompt.
Answer prompt questions.
Develop paragraphs.
Increase vocab.

Strategies: Conclusion

* 2-page minimum

homonyms
sent. fragments
appositives

After completion of the assessment task, don't forget to follow up!

In English Class:

1. Review the assignment.
2. If there was a prompt, review the key points that were to be addressed.
3. Model an exemplary response.
4. Based on the information derived from your Class Analysis Chart, reteach a skill that students are globally deficient in.
5. Give students opportunities to work on revision skills.

Strategy #1: Small Group Revision / Same Writing Sample

Groups of 4-5 students will work together in small groups to improve the same writing sample (on transparency, if possible). The goal will be to get it to a Score 6 in 10-15 minutes. A discussion leader will keep the group focused, making sure that all students participate. One student will write for the whole group. After writing, groups will present their revised piece. The rest of the class will score and discuss. The teacher will observe, listen, take notes, and participate in the discussion if asked by students.

Strategy #2: Partner Revision / Individual Writing Samples

Each student will trade papers with a partner, reading and scoring the partner's paper. Each partner will discuss weaknesses and offer suggestions for improvement. After ten minutes, partners will reread and evaluate.

In Content-area Classes:

1. Review the key points that were expected to be addressed.

1. Model an exemplary response.

3. Give students 10 minutes to revise their originals. Discuss, share, or read with a partner or in a small group. (These would not be reevaluated for a "second chance" score.)

4. If time permits, practice Revision Strategy #1 above.

Just  ™ It!

Checklist for Intermediate Revision

Focus on the Topic
Did I focus on the topic and not run away with other ideas?
Did I answer or address all the questions in the prompt?

Logical Order
Beginning
Did I use a lead to get my readers interested?
At the very least, did I mention the topic or title in my first paragraph?
Middle(s)
Is the body organized, probably by the questions in the prompt?
End
Is my conclusion more than one sentence?
Did I solve the problem, tell how things turned out, or review my main points?
Did I consider ending the piece with a reflection, opinion, or question?

Interesting Words/Challenging Vocabulary
Did I eliminate all overused words such as *went, said, big, little,* and *good*?

Different Sentence Patterns
Does my essay sound like a list?
Did I vary my sentence patterns, using questions, exclamations, and series?
Did I try to write longer, more complex sentences?
Do my sentence patterns contribute to overall fluency?

Exceptional Supporting Details
Did I give several examples that I explained in detail?
Did I use precise verbs?
Did I name people, places, and things with proper nouns?
Did I include adjectives – but not too many?
Did I try to create a clear vision for the reader?

Audience
Did I write for a specific audience?
Did my personality shine through my writing?

Just  ™ It!

Checklist for Advanced Revision

Focus on the Topic
Did I focus on the topic and not run away with other ideas?
Did I answer or address all the questions in the prompt?
If there were no questions, did I design my own questions?

Logical Order
Introduction
Did I use a lead to get my readers interested?
Did I develop a setting or give an overview of what I was going to write about?
At the very least, did I mention the topic or title in my first paragraph?
Body
Is the body organized, probably by the questions in the prompt?
Does each paragraph address a new question?
Conclusion
Is my conclusion more than one sentence?
Did I lead into the end of the story or essay?
Did I solve the problem, tell how things turned out, or review my main points?
Did I consider ending the piece with a reflection, opinion, or question?

Interesting Words/Challenging Vocabulary
Did I eliminate all overused words such as *went, said, big, little*, and *good*?
Did I go back and look for at least three more opportunities to use challenging vocabulary?
Are my new words used correctly?

Different Sentence Patterns
Did I vary my sentence patterns, using questions, exclamations, and items in a series?
Did I develop compound and/or complex sentences?
Did I remember to use prepositional phrases, adverbs, and participial phrases?
Do my sentences create smooth transitions and contribute to overall fluency?

Descriptive Sentences
Did I create a vision for the reader that included several detailed examples?
Did I use precise verbs?
Did I name people, places, and things with proper nouns?
Did I include adjectives – but not too many?
Did I incorporate other literary devices such as simile, metaphor, personification, etc. to create vivid descriptions?

Audience
Did I write for a specific audience?
Did my tone match the prompt?
Did my personality shine through my writing?

Tracking the Data

Who is in charge of the data collection and the progress updates?

There are two basic reasons for data collection:

1) classroom assessment for the purpose of a grade, and
2) information for a school improvement plan that provides proof that a specific goal was attempted, strategies were provided, and improvement was seen.

In the classroom setting, the teacher will obviously be the one collecting and interpreting the data for instructional use. For building or district-wide purposes, a writing chairperson or school administrator must be in charge of collecting, charting, and analyzing the data. If this is your responsibility, don't forget the importance of reporting back to teachers with the results. If teachers are expected to turn in quarterly data, then they are entitled to a quarterly written school-wide progress report or a brief update during a staff meeting. The most important thing to remember is that everyone's time is valuable!

Charts for Tracking Progress

Charts on the following pages are provided for school-wide data collection.

Quarterly Tracking Chart
This chart is intended for tracking the percentage of passing students in each class for baseline, quarterly, and final assessment. If the percentage is not consistently increasing, teachers should consider this as an indication that writing instruction needs more focus.

Self Evaluation Chart
This chart gives teachers an opportunity to self-evaluate, basically asking, "Have I really done this or not?" Subject integration is addressed, as well as the identification of weaknesses in certain classes or grade levels.

Yearly Class Record
Data from Class Analysis Charts is transferred to the Yearly Class Record for purposes of recording over-all improvement (for the school improvement plan documentation) or for copying and forwarding this student information on to the next year's English teacher.

QUARTERLY TRACKING CHART FOR WRITING PROGRESS

Local/Standardized

Task ______________ **Date** ________ **% Passing** _________

	# of Students	Score 0 N %	Score 1 N %	Score 2 N %	Score 3 N %	Score 4 N %	Score 5 N %	Score 6 N %
(6) Writing Application								
(4) Lang. Conventions								

Task ______________ **Date** ________ **% Passing** _________

	# of Students	Score 0 N %	Score 1 N %	Score 2 N %	Score 3 N %	Score 4 N %	Score 5 N %	Score 6 N %
(6) Writing Application								
(4) Lang. Conventions								

Task ______________ **Date** ________ **% Passing** _________

	# of Students	Score 0 N %	Score 1 N %	Score 2 N %	Score 3 N %	Score 4 N %	Score 5 N %	Score 6 N %
(6) Writing Application								
(4) Lang. Conventions								

TEACHER ________________________________ **GR. LEVEL** _____ **YEAR** ________

Secondary Teacher Reflection and Self-evaluation Using The Simple 6™ to Improve Writing Skills

COMPONENTS

Focus on the Topic: Great ___ OK ___ Didn't attempt ___
Notes:

Logical Order: Great ___ OK ___ Didn't attempt ___
Notes:

Challenging Vocabulary: Great ___ OK ___ Didn't attempt ___
Notes:

Sentence Patterns: Great ___ OK ___ Didn't attempt ___
Notes:

Supporting Details: Great ___ OK ___ Didn't attempt ___
Notes:

Audience: Great ___ OK ___ Didn't attempt ___
Notes:

FOLLOW UP

Modeled Exemplary Examples: Yes ___ No ___

Met with Flexible Groups: Yes ___ No ___

Taught mini-lessons for literary devices: Yes ___ No ___

IMPROVEMENT SEEN IN: ______________________________

____

STILL NEED TO FOCUS ON: ______________________________

____

YEARLY CLASS RECORD: WRITING PROMPTS

GRADES 6-12 Year: _____ Teacher: ____________________

STUDENT NAMES	BASELINE:AUG.	PROMPT 1:OCT.	PROMPT 2: JAN.	PROMPT 3:MAR.	FINAL: MAY
	CONT (6) /CONV (4)	CONT (6)/CONV (4)	CONT (6) / CONV (4)	CONT (6) /CONV (4)	CONT (6) /CONV (4)
% PASSING CONT./CONV.	/	/	/	/	/

Conclusion

The Simple 6™ helps students to focus on the elements of exemplary writing. The beauty is in the design – a simple analytic rubric that students as young as first or second grade can understand and explain to others. Teachers who have implemented the program are amazed at how little time it takes before seeing students who are confident and focused. Because they now have a clear understanding of what is expected, writing skills show improvement within the first few weeks.

The Simple 6™ is like anything else that we teach. If we don't continue to give students opportunities to write, they won't improve their skills. If we don't continue to model strategies, they will forget what is expected at the highest level. If we don't continue to encourage them, they will lose interest. If we don't continue to give them feedback, they won't be able to take advantage of our expertise. The alternative is – we must continue to analyze the data, present lessons with enthusiasm, tie writing lessons to students' interests and other content areas, stay on a consistent schedule throughout the entire year, and always ask, "Did you Simple 6™ it?"

Writing is a lifelong skill, and each teacher's contribution to their students' improvement and confidence is critical. *It doesn't matter if you're a six-year-old writing your first story, a sixteen-year-old taking the SAT, or an adult writing a note to your child's teacher. . .*

If you ***FOCUS ON THE TOPIC*** *in your writing, the reader will immediately know the purpose.*

If you structure your writing with ***LOGICAL ORDER****, the reader will be able to follow and understand your message.*

If you include ***CHALLENGING VOCABUARY****, you will sound as intelligent as you really are.*

If you develop ***VARIED SENTENCE PATTERNS****, your writing will be fluent and hold your reader's interest.*

If you include ***EXCEPTIONAL SUPPORTING DETAILS****, the reader will be able to clearly visualize the message you are trying to convey.*

If you connect with the ***AUDIENCE****, then what you have written has made an impact.*

Just Simple 6™ it!

Resources Read, Cited, or Recommended

Books in Print

Bohlke, Lara. *501 writing prompts.* New York: Learning Express. (2003)

Davidson, Kay. *Writing: the simple 6™.* Marion, IL: Pieces of Learning. (2003)

Indiana Department of Education. Indiana's academic standards. Indianapolis: Indiana Department of Education. (2006)

Sebranek, Patrick, Meyer, Verne, & Kemper, Dave. *Write source 2000.* New York: D.C. Heath. (1995)

Van Vickle, Linda. *Figurative language.* St. Louis: McDonald Publishing Company. (2004)

Zemelman, Steven & Daniels, Harvey. *A community of writers.* Portsmouth: Heinemann. (1988)

Warriner's high school handbook. Chicago: Holt, Rinehart and Winston, Inc. (1992)

Writer's companion: middle grades. Englewood Cliffs, NJ: Prentice Hall. (1995)

Web Sites

About Freelance Writing
http://www.aboutfreelancewriting.com/articles/howtosample/voice.htm

Cleveland State University: The Writing Center
http://www.csuohio.edu/writingcenter/introcnc.htm

Guide to Writing a Basic Essay
http://members.tripod.com/~lklivingston/essay/intro.htm

Introduction Strategies.
http://web.mit.edu/writing/Writing_Types/introstrategies.html

Kim's Korner for Teacher Talk
http://www.kimskorner4teachertalk.com/writing/voice/howto/html

Literary Devices
http://mrbraiman.home.att.net/lit.htm

Resources

Literacy Education Online
http://leo.stcloudstate.edu/acadwrite/conclude.html

Online Writing Lab
http://owl.english.purdue.edu/workshops/hypertext/ResearchW/writeintro.html

Teaching that makes sense: looking for quality in student writing
http://www.ttms.org/writing_quality/voice.htm

University Writing Center, The
http://www.uwc.ucf.edu/Writing%20Resources/Handouts/conclusions_ideas.html

Write away: finding your voice
http://www.efuse.com/Design/wa-voice.html

Write 101
http://www.write101.com/lethamfind.htm

Writing Center, The: University of North Carolina at Chapel Hill
http://www.unc.edu/depts/wcweb/handouts/conclusions.html